Lonely planet

LONELY PLANET'S
ULTIMATE
TRAVEL
QUIZ
BOOK
2

**MORE FIENDISH BRAIN-TEASERS
FROM EASY TO HARD**

CONTENTS

Introduction 4

Quiz 1:   Around the World in
          25 Countries 6
Quiz 2:   The World of Wildlife 8
Quiz 3:   North Africa 10
Quiz 4:   Festivals Around
          the World 12
Quiz 5:   Airports 14
Quiz 6:   USA 16
Quiz 7:   Rio de Janeiro 18
Quiz 8:   Northern Europe 20
Quiz 9:   Wonders of the World 22
Quiz 10: Silhouette Countries
          (*picture quiz*) 24

Quiz 11: General Travel Knowledge 26
Quiz 12: Central and East Asia 28
Quiz 13: London 30
Quiz 14: Bridges 32
Quiz 15: Waterfalls 34
Quiz 16: General Travel Knowledge 36
Quiz 17: South Africa 38
Quiz 18: Train Travel 40
Quiz 19: Central America 42
Quiz 20: Museums and Galleries 44

Quiz 21: Around the World in
          25 Capitals 46
Quiz 22: South America 48
Quiz 23: Japan 50
Quiz 24: Forests and Jungles 52
Quiz 25: Planes and Air Travel 54
Quiz 26: General Travel Knowledge 56

Quiz 27: Egypt 58
Quiz 28: Pacific Islands 60
Quiz 29: Languages 62
Quiz 30: World Landmarks
         (*picture quiz*) 64

Quiz 31: General Travel Knowledge 66
Quiz 32: Western Europe 68
Quiz 33: Religious Buildings 70
Quiz 34: The Amazon 72
Quiz 35: Australia 74
Quiz 36: General Travel Knowledge 76
Quiz 37: Boats and Ships 78
Quiz 38: The Caribbean 80
Quiz 39: Film Locations Around
         the World 82
Quiz 40: Seas and Oceans 84

Quiz 41: True or False? 86
Quiz 42: West Africa 88
Quiz 43: Castles, Palaces
         and Fortresses 90
Quiz 44: Sydney 92
Quiz 45: Deserts 94
Quiz 46: France 96
Quiz 47: The Wide World of Sports 98
Quiz 48: Explorers and Voyages
         of Discovery 100
Quiz 49: Southeast Asia 102
Quiz 50: Silhouette Cities
         (*picture quiz*) 104

Quiz 51: Guess the Country 106
Quiz 52: Central and
         Southern Africa 108

Quiz 53: Monuments
and Architecture 110
Quiz 54: New York 112
Quiz 55: Natural Wonders 114
Quiz 56: General Travel Knowledge 116
Quiz 57: Buses and Bikes 118
Quiz 58: China 120
Quiz 59: South Asia 122
Quiz 60: Food and Drink 124

Quiz 61: Around the World
in 25 Journeys 126
Quiz 62: The UK 128
Quiz 63: World Heritage Sites 130
Quiz 64: The Cities of Italy 132
Quiz 65: Volcanoes 134
Quiz 66: General Travel Knowledge 136
Quiz 67: Mexico 138
Quiz 68: Central and
Eastern Europe 140
Quiz 69: Money and Currencies 142
Quiz 70: What in the World?
(*picture quiz*) 144

Quiz 71: General Travel Knowledge 146
Quiz 72: Antarctica 148
Quiz 73: Dams Around the World 150
Quiz 74: Russia 152
Quiz 75: Rivers and Lakes 154
Quiz 76: General Travel Knowledge 156
Quiz 77: Car Travel 158
Quiz 78: New Zealand 160
Quiz 79: Southwest Europe 162
Quiz 80: The World of Literature 164

Quiz 81: Around the
Ancient World 166
Quiz 82: East Africa 168
Quiz 83: The World's
Tallest Buildings 170
Quiz 84: Beijing 172
Quiz 85: Roads and Routes 174
Quiz 86: General Travel
Knowledge 176
Quiz 87: National Parks 178
Quiz 88: Brazil 180
Quiz 89: The Middle East 182
Quiz 90: US Silhouette States
(*picture quiz*) 184

Quiz 91: General Travel
Knowledge 186
Quiz 92: Southeast Europe 188
Quiz 93: Mountains 190
Quiz 94: Germany 192
Quiz 95: International
Organisations 194
Quiz 96: General Travel
Knowledge 196
Quiz 97: Canada 198
Quiz 98: The World of Art 200
Quiz 99: The Arctic 202
Quiz 100: Borders Around
The World 204

ANSWERS 206

INTRODUCTION

BY JOE FULLMAN

Welcome back to the world of quizzing!

That's assuming that you've already bought and enjoyed the first title in this now growing series, *Lonely Planet's Ultimate Quiz Book*, henceforth to be known as *Lonely Planet's Ultimate Quiz Book 1*. And if you've yet to get a copy, consider this a reminder to put in an order.

For this second version, we've taken everything that was great about the first one and, though we say so ourselves, improved things just a little bit. As before, we're going to take an epic tour around the world of trivia – via 100 quizzes and more than 2000 questions – to see just how many fascinating facts are lodged in your brain (it's always many more than you think), but there are a few differences this time round.

Whereas the first book was split into Easy, Medium and Hard sections, this title does away with such artificial divisions – after all, one person's hard is another's easy; it just depends what's in your brain – to provide a mixture of difficulty levels in every quiz. There should be a good number of questions that make you go, 'Oh my word, how preposterously easy,' although do be sure to check the answers. Sometimes what looks obvious is nothing of the kind. Others will seem ridiculously hard, so obscure that perhaps they're not even worth attempting. But before you skip over, it's worth reading the question again. There's often a clue in there leading you down the right path. And many questions have multiple choice options, one of which is nearly always impossible, thus narrowing your chances to, at worst, a 50/50 bet. The majority of questions on the following pages are what we would term 'medium', although all these categories are really in the eye of the quiz beholder.

We've also widened our thematic approach with this new quizzing tome. The first book was fairly general in its scope. For this one, we've included many more themed rounds to allow us to really delve into subjects. All the quizzes fall under eight broadly travel-related categories – Regions, Countries, Cities, Travel & Transport, The Natural World, Landmarks & Buildings, Culture and Pot Luck – and, with those, we think we've pretty much got the whole world covered.

Many quizzes also have one or two picture-related questions, and there are a few dedicated picture rounds to help break up all the words.

So, with the approach to this second Lonely Planet quiz book explained, it's time to get down to business. And it can be a serious business. Answering trivia questions can seem inherently pointless, but what other idle mental pursuit gives you the chance to win large sums of money just for revealing what you know? Since television's earliest days, the quiz show has been a programming staple, often with big-money prizes involved. Arcane knowledge can have serious value. And nobody begrudges someone who scoops a tidy sum on a quiz show; that the winner has hordes of fiendishly obscure facts lodged in the inner recesses of their brain is considered impressive, a skill, and certainly something worthy of being handed a large sum of cash. Of course, the best most of us can hope for during our quizzing careers is a much smaller pot won at a pub quiz or at a 'friendly game' between work colleagues. But that can bring just as much satisfaction as a televisual triumph – sometimes even more so, depending on the work colleagues. For the record, we should state that there are no prizes available for getting the questions in this book right. Think of it more as a practice run for when your big day comes.

That also means there are no penalties for getting questions wrong. And, counter-intuitive as it may seem, getting things wrong is one of the other great joys of quizzing, as it involves learning new things, which can either be stored away to be brought out at another quiz or just casually crowbarred into conversation to amaze your lucky friends. That's the thing about knowledge; it needs to be shared, and the quiz is one of the best ways of passing around information that we've come up with.

This is a book to be enjoyed in multiple settings: on your own (testing yourself against yourself, perhaps sat in an armchair or at an airport waiting for a connection), with friends and family, or maybe even at a work event with those colleagues. But wherever and however you do it, remember the same rules apply: no phones, no cheating. Happy quizzing!

Quiz 1 **Around the World in 25 Countries**

Let's start with a quick tour around the world.
Every answer is a different country (or countries).

1. Which country's provinces include Alberta and Manitoba?

2. The Galápagos Islands belong to which South American country?
   A) Ecuador **B)** Chile **C)** Brazil

3. In what African country would you find the rock-hewn churches of Lalibela
   A) South Africa **B)** Angola **C)** Ethiopia

4. The coastal city of Montego Bay is in which Caribbean country?
   A) Cuba **B)** Jamaica **C)** Trinidad

5. Which of these Asian countries is *not* landlocked?
   A) Nepal **B)** Bhutan **C)** Pakistan

6. In which country might you be served a cake called a lamington?
   A) Australia **B)** USA **C)** France

7. Which country is the world's largest producer of gold?
   A) South Africa **B)** China **C)** Australia

8. The Øresund Bridge links which two European countries?

9. Where would you find La Rinconada, the world's highest permanent settlement, located around 5100m (16,000ft) above sea level?
   A) Bangladesh **B)** Austria **C)** Peru

10. The kiwi is the national animal of which country?

11. If you wanted to see the great zebra herds of the Serengeti National Park, which African country should you visit?
    A) Kenya **B)** Tanzania **C)** Algeria

12. São Paolo is the largest city of which South American country?

13. In *The Lost Continent*, travel writer Bill Bryson recalls a journey around the small towns of which country?
A) Australia B) UK C) USA

14. The family of birds known as 'birds of paradise', famed for their dazzling plumage, are mainly found in which country?

15. The territory that lies on the east coast of South America, with Suriname to the west and Brazil to the south and east is an overseas department of which European country?

16. In North Africa, what is the only country that has a land border with both Algeria and Egypt?

17. In which of the UK's four constituent countries would you find the Old Course at St Andrews, the oldest golf course in the world?

18. Tirana is the capital of which European country?

19. The sport of *Tejo*, which involves throwing metal discs at small targets packed with gunpowder, is a popular sport in which country?
A) Colombia B) Kenya C) Samoa

20. The volcano of Krakatoa, which erupted spectacularly in 1883, lies in which Southeast Asian country?

21. The five coldest cities on Earth are all in which country?
A) Canada B) Norway C) Russia

22. Covering an area of less than 0.5 sq km (0.2 sq miles), what is the smallest country in the world?

23. Which of these countries is located on the Horn of Africa?
A) Morocco B) Somalia C) Namibia

24. The złoty is the currency of which European country?

25. Which of these countries is not crossed by the Equator?
A) Ecuador B) Kenya C) Argentina

Quiz 2 **The World of Wildlife**

1. *Mephitis mephitis* is the scientific name for which iconic, and rather smelly, North American animal?

2. This coat belongs to which big cat?
   A) A jaguar from South America
   B) A leopard from Africa
   C) A tiger from Asia

3. Found leaping across the European Alps, the ibex is a type of what animal?
   A) Deer B) Sheep C) Goat

4. What is the only type of mammal native to New Zealand?

5. Pandas are a type of vegetarian bear. True or false?

6. What is the name given to the type of sharks that spend much of their time hidden on the seabed?
   A) Carpet sharks B) Plate sharks C) Seafloor sharks

7. The wisent is the European version of which animal, also found in North America?

8. What type of animal is a mola?
   A) Reptile B) Mammal C) Fish

9. What is the only country outside of Africa to have a wild population of lions?
   A) Saudi Arabia B) China C) India

10. The giant anteater is native to which continent?
    A) Europe B) South America C) Africa

11. What colour is a giraffe's tongue?
    A) Purple B) Green C) Yellow with brown spots

12. Found on just a couple of islands in Indonesia, what is the largest lizard in the world?

13. What type of animal is a quokka?
    A) A giant rodent from South America
    B) A nocturnal carnivore from Asia
    C) A small marsupial from Australia

14. What is the largest species of dolphin?

15. The South American capybara is the largest what in the world?
    A) Snake B) Rodent C) Flightless bird

16. What is the world's largest land predator?
    A) Siberian tiger B) African lion C) Polar bear

17. The springbok is the national animal of which African country?

18. African elephants are not just the largest living land animal, they also have the longest pregnancy. On average, how long does it last?
    A) 11 months B) 22 months C) 33 months

19. The national animal of two Central American countries, the turquoise-browed motmot is what sort of animal? And, for two bonus points, can you name those two countries?
    A) Bird B) Reptile C) Fish

20. What is unusual about the way hippos poo?
    A) They do it standing on their hind legs
    B) They can only do it underwater
    C) They spin their tails to scatter the poo as it comes out

Quiz 3 **North Africa**

1. The Sahara Desert covers how much of the African continent?
    A) 11% B) 21% C) 31%

2. What, literally, does the word 'Sahara' mean?
    A) Desert B) Sandy C) Oasis

3. How many humps do the dromedary camels of North Africa have?

4. What is the capital of Morocco?

5. In what country would you find the northernmost point in Africa?

6. What is the most commonly spoken language in North Africa?

7. Which North African country is, by area, the largest country on the whole continent?

8. What is this traditional North African cooking dish called?

9. What is the name of the North African nomadic people who traditionally wear blue clothing?

10. Found in many ancient North African cities, what is a casbah?
    A) Fortress B) Tea shop C) Spice market

11. In what year did the Arab Spring revolts begin in North Africa?
    A) 2006 B) 2011 C) 2016

12. At their closest point across the Straits of Gibraltar, how far away are the continents of Europe and Africa?
A) 1.4km (0.9 miles) B) 14km (9 miles) C) 140km (90 miles)

13. What are the countries either side of this closest point?

14. What is the name of the hot, dusty wind that regularly blows from North Africa across the Mediterranean into southern Europe?
A) Chinook B) Mistral C) Sirocco

15. The ruins of the city of Carthage, which in ancient times controlled a great Mediterranean empire, can be found in what modern North African country?

16. The national animal of Algeria, what is this cute little creature?

17. Which mountain range stretches across much of the northwest part of the region?
A) Ural Mountains B) Atlas Mountains C) Great Dividing Range

18. What is the name of the semi-arid region of shrubland and grasslands just to south of the Sahara?

19. What is an erg?
A) A large flat area of sand in a desert
B) A dish made with cous cous, lamb and figs
C) A traditional dance performed at weddings

20. By population, what is the largest city in North Africa?

Quiz 4 Festivals Around the World

1. The huge Oktoberfest beer-drinking festival is mainly celebrated in which German city?

2. New Orleans marks the festival of Mardi Gras with parades and dancing in the run-up to Easter, but what does Mardi Gras literally mean?
   A) Sad grass B) Fat Tuesday C) March madness

3. What yellow flowers are particularly associated with Mexico's Day of the Dead festival?

4. And in what month is the Day of the Dead celebrated?

5. Europe's largest annual carnival is centred on which multicultural London district, famed for its market?

6. When is Australia Day, the official national day of Australia?

7. The Venice Biennale is one of world's most prestigious arts festivals. How often is it held?
   A) Twice a year B) Every year C) Every two years

8. The Maralal International Camel Derby is held annually in which African country?
   A) Morocco B) Mali C) Kenya

9. What gift is traditionally given to children at Chinese New Year?
   A) Coal in a black bag
   B) Money in a red envelope
   C) A jade statue in a green box

10. The Fritto Misto Festival in Ascoli Piceno, Italy, celebrates what?
    A) Fried Food B) Friendship C) Friday nights

11. The traditional 'big three' international film festivals are held in Venice, Cannes and what other European city?

12. What is the name of the main seated venue for the Rio de Janeiro Carnival, through which the elaborate floats, costumed dancers and musicians parade?
A) Rumbaroom B) Sambadrome C) Salsastadium

13. A special nine-branch menorah, or candle holder, is lit during which Jewish festival?

14. Fuji Rock is a music festival in which country?

15. In what four cities are the 'Big Four' fashion weeks held?
You get a point for each

16. The dot in the below image marks the rough location of the venue for which annual music festival?

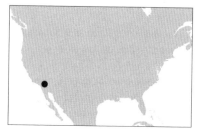

17. Celebrating the peoples and cultures of the Pacific islands, in what country is the annual Pasifika Festival held?
A) Tonga B) Samoa C) New Zealand

18. On what date does Ireland, and Irish communities around the world, celebrate the day of their patron saint, St Patrick?

19. In what year was the first Glastonbury Music Festival held?
A) 1960 B) 1970 C) 1980

20. By what name is the carnival-like harvest festival held every year in Barbados known?
A) Crop Over B) Planting Past C) Grown 'n' Gone

- 13 - Score

Quiz 5 **Airports**

1. DEL is the airport code for which city's international airport?
   For an extra point, what politician, the country's prime minister in
   the 1970s and 80s, is it named after?

2. Charles de Gaulle, Orly and Beauvais are the three main airports
   for which European city?

3. What is Australia's busiest international airport?
   A) Sydney B) Melbourne C) Perth

4. KIN is the airport code for which city's international airport?
   A) Kinshasa, Democratic Republic of Congo
   B) Karachi, Pakistan
   C) Kingston, Jamaica

5. The world's busiest airport is located in which US city?
   A) New York B) Atlanta C) Los Angeles

6. The world's first purpose-built airport terminal was constructed
   in the 1920s at which London airport?
   A) Heathrow B) Gatwick C) Croydon

7. What is unusual about Gisborne Airport in New Zealand?
   A) It's submerged beneath the sea for several hours a day
   B) It has a railway line that cuts across the runway
   C) It can be retracted under the ground when not in use

8. BKK is the airport code for which city's main international
   airport? For an extra two points, what is the airport's name?

9. Where would you find the world's largest airport terminal building?
   A) Beijing, China B) Dubai, UAE C) London Heathrow

10. What is the total length of the baggage conveyor belts at Dubai
    International Airport?
    A) 7km (4.3 miles) B) 175km (109 miles) C) 350 (217 miles)

11. Singapore Changi Airport is home to a tropical bird aviary, which travellers can visit while awaiting their flight.
True or false?

12. College Park Airport in Maryland, USA, holds what claim to fame?
    A) It is the world's oldest continuously operated airport
    B) It's the world's highest airport
    C) It's the only airport located entirely underground

13. JNB is the airport code for which city's international airport?
For an extra two points, what is the airport's name?

14. Batman is an airport in which country?
    A) USA B) Turkey C) China

15. O'Hare International in Chicago, USA has the largest number of runways of any airport. But how many exactly is that?
    A) 6 B) 7 C) 8

16. The busiest airport in Asia is in which country?
    A) China B) Japan C) United Arab Emirates

17. In 2016, the main airport on the Portuguese island of Madeira was renamed in honour of what locally born football hero?

18. In what African country would you find Jomo Kenyatta International Airport?
    A) South Africa B) Senegal C) Kenya

19. Salzburg Airport in Austria is named after which famous classical composer, who was born in the city in 1756?
    A) Beethoven B) Wagner C) Mozart

20. Serving the city of New York, USA, Idlewild Airport was renamed what in 1963?

Quiz 6 USA

1. What is the national bird of the USA?

2. In 1959, what territory became the 50th US state?
   A) Hawaii B) Alaska C) Puerto Rico

3. What is the official name of the US national anthem?

4. What is the name of the river that forms the border between the capital, Washington, DC, and the state of Virginia?

5. Name the five US states with borders on the Pacific. You get a point for each.

6. Erected in the capital in the 19th century to honour the country's first president, the Washington Monument has at its tip a cap made of what metal?
   A) Gold B) Silver C) Aluminium

7. What southern city was the capital of the Confederacy during the Civil War?

8. What is the tallest building in the USA?
   A) Central Park Tower B) One World Trade Center C) Willis Tower

9. A speciality of New Orleans, what sort of dish is gumbo?
   A) A stew B) A sandwich C) A salad

10. How many US states have just four letters in their name?

11. Which of these is the name of a major league baseball team based in Dallas?
    A) Texas Rangers B) Dallas Mavericks C) Houston Texans

12. What was the name the 19th-century female abolitionist who is believed to have rescued at least 70 enslaved people using a network of safe houses known as the Underground Railroad?

13. Who was the US author of numerous California-set works, including *Of Mice and Men*, *East of Eden* and *Cannery Row*?

14. Mount Rushmore, shown below, displays the likenesses of four US presidents: George Washington, Thomas Jefferson, Abraham Lincoln and who else?
    A) Martin Van Buren
    B) Theodore Roosevelt
    C) Franklin Delano Roosevelt

15. For two points, how many stars and how many stripes are there on the US flag?

16. By population, New York is the biggest city in the USA, but what is the second most populous?
    A) Chicago B) Los Angeles C) Miami

17. The USA is home to four large deserts: the Great Basin Desert, the Sonoran Desert, the Chihuahuan Desert and which other desert located in the country's southwest?

18. One of the residents of those southwestern deserts, the gila monster is what sort of creature?
    A) Poisonous lizard B) Burrowing mammal C) Flightless bird

19. Also known as the 'Great White Way', what is the name of the New York street that lies at the heart of the city's theatre district?

20. By area, what is the smallest state in the USA?
    A) Connecticut B) Delaware C) Rhode Island

Quiz 7 **Rio de Janeiro**

1. In what century was Rio de Janeiro founded?
   A) 12th B) 16th C) 20th

2. In what year did Rio host the Summer Olympic Games?
   A) 1936 B) 1984 C) 2016

3. What is the name of the main river ('*rio*' in Portuguese) that flows through the centre of the city?
   A) Janeiro B) Amazon C) There isn't one

4. What is the name of Rio's football stadium, once the biggest in the world, where the finals of the 1950 and 2014 World Cups were held?
   A) Maracanã B) Santiago Bernabeu C) La Bombonera

5. How many days does the city's famous carnival last?
   A) One B) Three C) Five

6. Which type of music is most closely associated with carnival?
   A) Samba B) Rumba C) Jazz

7. What is the name of this mountain, which overlooks the city?
   A) Table Mountain B) Sugar Loaf Mountain C) Ojos del Salado

8. In the early 19th century, Rio de Janeiro was briefly the capital of Portugal. True or false?

9. In what year did Rio de Janeiro cease to be Brazil's capital?
   A) 1860 B) 1960 C) 2000

10. By what nickname are the residents of Rio de Janeiro known?
    A) Cariocas B) Rioestas C) Janeiro-heroes

11. What part of the Brazilian flag is supposed to represent
    Rio de Janeiro?
    A) The diamond B) The circle C) The stars

12. What is the name of the 'new wave' music that emerged in
    Rio de Janeiro in the 1950s and 60s, as featured in songs
    such as 'The Girl from Ipanema'.

13. How tall is the statue of Christ the Redeemer (*Cristo Redentor*)
    that overlooks the city?
    A) 10m (33ft) B) 30m (98ft) C) 300m (328ft)

14. What is the name of the mountain on which it stands?
    A) Corcovado B) Pedra da Gávea C) Morro Dois Irmãos

15. What is the 4km (2.5 mile) stretch of sandy beach in the city's
    South Zone that shares its name with a Barry Manilow song?

16. What is the name of bay on which Rio de Janeiro is situated
    A) Samborombón Bay B) Bay of Biscay C) Guanabara Bay

17. What is the name of the science museum on Rio's waterfront?
    A) The Museum of Yesterday
    B) The Museum of Today
    C) The Museum of Tomorrow

18. Who were the original native inhabitants of the Rio area?
    A) The Tupi B) The Maya C) The Inca

19. In the 19th century, farms around Rio de Janeiro successfully
    swapped from farming sugar to farming which crop?
    A) Cotton B) Coffee C) Brazil nuts

20. In what year was Rio designated a World Heritage Site by UNESCO?
    A) 1912 B) 1962 C) 2012

Quiz 8 **Northern Europe**

1. What is the name of the Scandinavian people who set out on missions of colonisation across much of Europe between the eighth and the eleventh centuries?

2. What is the capital of Finland?

3. Can you name the island that appeared out of the sea off the coast of Iceland in 1963 following a period of intense volcanic activity?

4. Often seen in the sky in the far north of Europe, the Aurora Borealis are more commonly known as what?

5. The archipelago of Svalbard in the Arctic Circle is home to the world's largest scientific collection of what?
   A) Ice samples B) Polar bear droppings C) Seeds

6. To which northern European country does Svalbard belong?
   A) Norway B) Sweden C) Finland

7. What name is given to the long, narrow inlets on Norway's coast formed by glaciers during the last ice age?

8. Which of the Baltic states is largest in terms of both area and population?
   A) Latvia B) Lithuania C) Estonia

9. From their nest sites in Iceland, which bird is known to undertake the world's longest migration, down to the Antarctic and back again, a distance that can exceed 70,000km (40,000 miles)?

10. The Baltic region is home to the world's largest reserves of what prehistoric material?
    A) Amber B) Dinosaur bones C) Coal

11. The 'Wife Carrying World Championship' has been held every year since 1997 in which northern European country?
    A) Sweden B) Finland C) Estonia

12. The Danish capital, Copenhagen, boasts a statue of what famous character from the stories of local author, Hans Christian Andersen?

13. A Swedish dish, celebrated for its intensely pungent aroma, *Surströmming* is made of what?
    A) Fermented fish B) Pickled reindeer meat C) Dried whale skin

14. Iceland sits on what tectonic boundary?
    A) Mid-Atlantic Ridge B) San Andreas Fault C) East Pacific Rise

15. What is the name of the nomadic people who herd reindeer in the far reaches of Norway, Sweden, Finland and Russia?

16. Hygge, the concept of contented cosiness, is particularly associated with which Scandinavian country?

17. What is the name of the sea ringed in the image below?
    A) Swedish Sea B) Norwegian Sea C) Baltic Sea

18. Iceland is home to the Althing, the world's oldest surviving parliament. In what year was it founded?
    A) 30 CE B) 930 CE C) 1930 CE

19. Which Scandinavian capital city was known as Kristiania until 1925?
    A) Copenhagen B) Stockholm C) Oslo

20. What temporary structure is set up every year in the town of Jukkasjärvi in northern Sweden?
    A) An ice hotel
    B) A polar bear feeding camp
    C) A base camp for travellers heading to the North Pole

Quiz 9 **Wonders of the World**

1. Of the original list of the Seven Wonders of the Ancient World, first compiled in second century BCE, which is the only wonder for which no physical evidence has ever been found?

2. One of the ancient wonders was a giant statue of which god, located at Olympia?
   A) Zeus B) Poseidon C) Apollo

3. The Colossus of Rhodes was a giant what?
   A) Statue B) Arena C) Ship

4. The Temple of Artemis was located in which ancient city?
   A) Athens B) Ephesus C) Carthage

5. Which is the only one of the original Seven Wonders of the Ancient World that is still standing?

6. In which modern country was the Mausoleum of Halicarnassus?
   A) Greece B) France C) Turkey

7. In 1994, the American Society of Civil Engineers came up with a new list, the Seven Wonders of the Modern World. Can you name the artificial waterway, completed in 1914, which featured on it?

8. South America's only representative was the Itaipu Dam, which stands on the border of Paraguay and which other country?

9. Can you name this North American entry from the list?

10. The Channel Tunnel between England and France also made the list. In what year did it open?
A) 1984 B) 1994 C) 2004

11. The other European entry on the list is an enormous flood protection system in which country?

12. In a 1933 film, the Empire State Building, which also made the list, was climbed by which fictional monster, referred to in the movie as the 'eighth wonder of the world'?

13. In 2007, an organisation called the New7Wonders Foundation issued an updated list called the New Seven Wonders of the World. Can you name the only one located in Europe? It's an arena built in the 1st century CE.

14. Can you name the most recent wonder on the new list, a statue erected in South America in the 1930s?

15. The other South American entry on the new list is the Inca fortress of Machu Picchu in Peru. In what century was it built?
A) 5th century BCE B) 5th century CE C) 15th century CE

16. And in what century was it rediscovered?
A) 18th B) 19th C) 20th

17. The Mexican entry on the new list, the ceremonial city of Chichen Itza, was built by which people?
A) The Aztecs B) The Maya C) The Olmecs

18. The only Middle Eastern entry on the new list is the ancient 'rose red' city of Petra. In what country is it located?

19. Can you name the 'wonder' on the new list that is over 21,000km (13,000 miles) long?

20. The Taj Mahal in India also features on the new list. What purpose was it built for?
A) As a tomb B) As a temple C) As an observatory

Quiz 10 **Silhouette Countries**

Can you identify which countries these silhouettes
represent from the three available options?

1.

A) USA B) Australia C) Algeria

2.

A) Brazil B) Morocco C) South Korea

3.

A) Greece B) Nicaragua C) Egypt

4.

A) Japan B) Indonesia C) Fiji

5.

A) Nicaragua B) Mexico C) Greece

6.

A) Bolivia B) Spain C) Afghanistan

7.

8.

A) Madagascar B) Sri Lanka C) Qatar   A) Chile B) Sweden C) Philippines

9.

10.

A) Peru B) Poland C) Kenya

A) Vietnam B) Lithuania C) Namibia

11.

12.

A) France B) New Zealand C) Latvia   A) Senegal B) Colombia C) Norway

13.
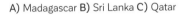

14.

A) Germany B) Uruguay C) Togo

A) Canada B) China C) Russia

15.

A) Mongolia
B) Turkey
C) Guatemala

Quiz 11 **General Travel Knowledge**

1. What is the grimly named area of California, USA, where the hottest ever air temperature of 56.7°C (134.1°F) was recorded?

2. According to legend, what were the names of the brothers who founded Rome?

3. At 830m (2722ft), the Burj Khalifa is the world's tallest building. In what Middle Eastern city is it located?
    A) Mecca, Saudi Arabia B) Baghdad, Iraq C) Dubai, UAE

4. What famous explorer gave the Pacific Ocean its name?
    A) Columbus B) Magellan C) Roald Amundsen

5. The coldest temperature ever recorded on Earth, −89.2°C (-128.6°F) was measured where?
    A) Siberia, Russia B) Antarctica C) The bottom of the ocean

6. What is the name of the name of this art gallery located in the Spanish capital, Madrid?

7. What is the world's longest (above-water) mountain range?
    A) Andes B) Alps C) Himalayas

8. What is the currency of Japan?

9. How many stars are there on the New Zealand flag?
    A) Three B) Four C) Five

10. What is the most commonly spoken language in China?
    A) Mandarin B) Cantonese C) English

11. Greenland forms part of the kingdom of which European nation?

12. By what name was Ho Chi Minh City, the largest city in Vietnam, formerly known?

13. What is the largest city in North America, by population?
    A) New York City B) Mexico City C) Toronto

14. In what country would you find Mount Kilimanjaro?
    A) Kenya B) Tanzania C) Egypt

15. Celebrated widely in India by Hindus, Buddhists, Jains and Sikhs, by what name is the Festival of Lights also known?

16. Australia's Shark Bay is home to the world's largest population of which marine mammals?
    A) Bottlenose dolphins B) Humpback whales C) Dugongs

17. What is the local name for the rolling grasslands of southern Africa?
    A) Veld B) Steppe C) Prairie

18. What is the only continent where you can find all 21 species of armadillo living in the wild?

19. The annual independent Sundance Film Festival is held in which US state?
    A) New York B) California C) Utah

20. What was the name of the architect who designed St Paul's Cathedral in London?

Quiz 12 **Central and East Asia**

1. In Central Asia, there are seven countries whose name ends in 'stan' (Afghanistan, Kazakhstan, Kyrgyzstan, Pakistan, Tajikistan, Turkmenistan and Uzbekistan), a Farsi word meaning what?
   A) Land B) People C) Mountains

2. Which of the seven countries is the largest by area?

3. Can you name the desert that covers almost 30% of Mongolia?

4. On land that has been leased to Russia, the purpose-built city of Baikonur in Kazakhstan is home to what major transport hub?
   A) A spaceport for launching rockets
   B) Central Asia's largest cruise ship port
   C) The first stop on the Trans-Siberian Railway

5. In what year did Seoul, the capital of South Korea, host the Olympic Games?
   A) 1968 B) 1988 C) 2008

6. *Qurutob*, also known as 'bread salad' is a dish from which central Asian country?
   A) Afghanistan B) Kyrgyzstan C) Tajikistan

7. What is the name of the 508m (1667ft) skyscraper in Taiwan that was briefly the world's largest? (Clue: its name describes its location and its number of storeys.)

8. Ashgabat is the capital of which central Asian country?

9. Used widely in Mongolia, what kind of object is a ger?
   A) A horse-drawn carriage B) A camel saddle C) A tent

10. With an average of just two people per sq km (5 people per sq mile), which Asian country is the least densely populated on Earth?
    A) Kazakhstan B) Mongolia C) China

11. Hyundai is a car company headquartered in which Asian country?

12. What is the longest river in China?

13. The ancient city of Samarkand is in which Central Asian country?
    A) Kyrgyzstan B) Turkmenistan C) Uzbekistan

14. What is the nickname of the Darvaza Crater, a natural gas field
    that's been burning continuously in Turkmenistan since 1971?
    A) Devil's Cauldron B) Gates of Hell C) Twisted Fire Starter

15. These statues depict the former leaders of which Asian country?

16. What was the name of the trade route that operated between the
    2nd century BCE and the Middle Ages, linking China with Europe
    via Central Asia?

17. What is plov, the national dish of Uzbekistan?
    A) A stew of rice, meat and vegetables
    B) Oven-baked lake fish
    C) A wheat cake flavoured with saffron

18. In 2019, Kazakhstan's capital changed its name from Astana to what?

19. The best known and best preserved sections of the Great Wall of
    China were built during which dynasty?
    A) Tang B) Ming C) Qing

20. In what year did North Korea and South Korea sign a peace treaty
    following the Korean War?
    A) 1953 B) 2003 C) They never have

Quiz 13 **London**

1. Completed in 1710 and standing 111m (364ft) tall, St Paul's Cathedral remained the tallest building in London until what year?
    A) 1863 B) 1963 C) 2013

2. What is now the tallest building in London?
    A) The Shard B) One Canada Square C) The Leadenhall Building

3. The ceremonial guardians of the Tower of London, officially known as Yeoman Warders, are also popularly known by what name?

4. What London museum is this?
    A) Natural History Museum B) British Museum C) Science Museum

5. What colour is the Victoria Line on the Tube map?
    A) Yellow B) Red C) Blue

6. What structure was built to hold the Great Exhibition of 1851?
    A) Alexandra Palace B) Lambeth Palace C) The Crystal Palace

7. Now a major shopping and entertainment hub, the London district of Covent Garden was until 1974 home to what?
    A) A fruit, vegetable and flower market
    B) A prison
    C) A royal palace

8. Platform 9 ¾, from which Harry Potter caught the Hogwarts Express, is supposedly located at which London train station?
    A) Liverpool Street B) King's Cross C) Paddington

9. In what royal park would you find London Zoo?
   A) Hyde Park B) Regent's Park C) Green Park

10. Traditionally, what colour are London's buses?

11. The giant Ferris wheel known as the London Eye was opened
    to commemorate which event?
    A) The Millennium
    B) The London Olympics
    C) The Queen's Diamond Jubilee

12. On which major square would you find the National Gallery?
    A) Trafalgar Square B) Leicester Square C) Soho Square

13. Big Ben is the name of the bell, but what is the name of the
    clock tower that contains it?
    A) Also Big Ben B) The Elizabeth Tower C) The Monument

14. In what year was the Great Fire of London?

15. What is the official name of the Houses of Parliament?
    A) The Palace of Westminster
    B) Buckingham Palace
    C) The Old Bailey

16. What is the major airport that lies to the south of Greater London?
    A) Heathrow B) Gatwick C) Stansted

17. The group of early 20th-century British writers that included
    Virginia Woolf, E.M. Forster and Lytton Strachey was named
    after which London district?

18. On what famous London shopping street would you find the
    department store, Selfridges?

19. Lords is a major international venue for which sport?

20. What famous luxury hotel on the Strand sits next to a theatre
    bearing the same name?

Quiz 14 **Bridges**

1. Approximately how many bridges are there in the canal-filled city of Venice?
   A) 40 B) 400 C) 4000

2. New York's Brooklyn Bridge spans the East River connecting Brooklyn to which of the city's other boroughs?

3. What is the name of the famous bridge in London which has decks that raise up to let tall ships past through?

4. Opened in 2022, where is the world's longest suspension bridge?
   A) USA B) Nigeria C) Turkey

5. In 1781, the British engineer Abraham Darby III constructed the first bridge made out of what material?
   A) Cast iron B) Gold C) Plastic

6. In what country would you find the longest bridge in the world?
   A) Brazil B) China C) Russia

7. What is the name of this statue-lined medieval bridge in the capital of the Czech Republic, Prague?
   A) Charles Bridge B) Henry Bridge C) Ferdinand Bridge

8. How many bridges are there across the Amazon River?
   A) 0 B) 10 C) 100

9. In what South African city would you find Nelson Mandela Bridge?

10. What is the official colour of San Francisco's Golden Gate Bridge?
    A) Domestic Red B) Solar Scarlet C) International Orange

11. The Romans build the first bridge in London across the River
    Thames in the 1st century CE. In what century was the river's
    second crossing, Westminster Bridge, built?
    A) 6th century B) 12th century C) 18th century

12. Linking Manhattan in New York City with New Jersey across the
    Hudson River, what is the busiest bridge in the world?

13. What sort of crossing is Scotland's Forth Bridge?
    A) A rail bridge B) A road bridge C) A pedestrian bridge

14. In what decade of the 20th century was the iconic Sydney
    Harbour Bridge completed?

15. The Ponte Vecchio is a medieval bridge in what Italian city?
    A) Milan B) Florence C) Rome

16. The 6th October Bridge is the longest bridge in Africa. In what
    country would you find it?
    A) Egypt B) Zambia C) Botswana

17. Spanning China's Beipan River, just how high is the Duge Bridge,
    the world's highest bridge?
    A) 365m (1198ft) B) 565m (1854ft) C) 865m (2838ft)

18. The Laguna Garzón Bridge in Uruguay is what unusual shape?
    A) Circular B) Triangular C) Star shaped

19. The Millau Viaduct in France holds what claim to fame?
    A) It's the world's oldest continuously used bridge
    B) It's the world's tallest bridge
    C) It's the world's shortest bridge

20. The current London Bridge replaced a 19th-century structure
    in the 1970s, which was sold to a US entrepreneur who had it
    dismantled and rebuilt at Lake Havasu City, in which US state?

Quiz 15 **Waterfalls**

1. How tall is the world's highest waterfall, Angel Falls?
   A) 579m (1900ft) B) 779m (2556ft) C) 979m (3212ft)

2. And in what country are the falls located?
   A) Canada B) Venezuela C) Nepal

3. The falls are named after Jimmie Angel, the American explorer who first brought them to international attention. In what decade of the 20th century did he discover the falls, and, for a bonus point, what form of transport was he using?

4. In what country would you find the world's second-highest waterfall, Tugela Falls?
   A) South Africa B) Australia C) Norway

5. Victoria Falls tumble over a section of which African river?
   A) Nile B) Limpopo C) Zambezi

6. Iguazu Falls lie on the border of Brazil and which other South American country?

7. The largest of the falls that make up Iguazu Falls is known as the Devil's what?
   A) Horns B) Throat C) Belly

8. Niagara Falls is actually made up of three separate falls: Horseshoe Falls, American Falls and what other falls?
   A) Best Man Falls B) Bridal Veil Falls C) Ring Bearer Falls

9. Who was the main female star of the 1953 Hollywood film-noir thriller, *Niagara*?
   A) Bette Davis B) Jane Russell C) Marilyn Monroe

10. What is special about the Marmore Falls in Umbria, Italy?
    A) They glow in the dark
    B) They are man-made
    C) They are only 20cm (8 inches) high

11. At 305m (1001ft) high, Wallaman Falls are the tallest waterfall in which country?
    A) Australia B) New Zealand C) Fiji

12. What is special about the waterfall at Malham Cove in North Yorkshire, England?
    A) It flows underground and can only be viewed from a cave
    B) It flowed for the first time in nearly 200 years in 2015
    C) Iron in the surrounding rocks turns the water bright red

13. At 773m (2536ft), Mongefossen is the tallest waterfall in Europe. In which Scandinavian country would you find it?
    A) Norway B) Sweden C) Finland

14. In which US state would you find Upside Down Falls, where strong winds regularly blow the water up into the air, making it look as if the falls are flowing in reverse?
    A) Alaska B) California C) Hawaii

15. Europe's widest waterfall, the Venta Rapid, is in which country?
    A) Spain B) Latvia C) Bulgaria

16. The name of the Welsh waterfall Sgwd Yr Eira translates as what?
    A) Fall of Mist B) Fall of Water C) Fall of Snow

17. In what Central American country are the Pulhapanzak Falls?
    A) Costa Rica B) Honduras C) Nicaragua

18. By what name is the waterfall in Colorado, USA, that regularly freezes in winter known?
    A) The Fang B) The Horn C) The Narwhal's Tusk

19. The Rio Damajagua Falls are a collection of 27 waterfalls in which Caribbean country?
    A) Jamaica B) Cuba C) The Dominican Republic

20. The Ekom–Nkam waterfalls are a pair of twin falls that seem to burst out of the jungle canopy in which African country?
    A) Cameroon B) Egypt C) The Gambia

Quiz 16 General Travel Knowledge

1. One of the world's smallest countries, San Marino is entirely
    surrounded by which other country?
    A) Austria B) Argentina C) Italy

2. What is the only Central American country to have English as
    its official language?
    A) Costa Rica B) Belize C) Panama

3. First produced in the 12th century, Commandaria is the world's
    oldest named wine still in production. In what country is it made?
    A) Cyprus B) Hungary C) Germany

4. A cloth produced on the Pacific islands of Tonga, Samoa and
    Fiji, what is *tapa* made from?
    A) Grass B) Cotton C) Tree bark

5. In what country was the Cuban revolutionary Ernesto 'Che'
    Guevara born?
    A) Cuba B) Argentina C) Bolivia

6. What is the currency of Eritrea?
    A) Eritrean nakfa B) Eritrean pound C) Eritrean rand

7. The autonomous region of Macau in China was formerly a
    colony of which European country?
    A) UK B) Spain C) Portugal

8. What does *Odlar Yurdu*, the motto of Azerbaijan mean?
    A) Land of Mountains B) Land of Plenty C) Land of Fire

9. The singer Björk is from which country?

10. Southern Rhodesia is a former name of which African country?
    A) Zimbabwe B) Lesotho C) Zambia

11. Northern Rhodesia is a former name of which African country?
    A) Zimbabwe B) Lesotho C) Zambia

12. The Pantanal, the world's largest tropical wetland, covers portions of Brazil, Paraguay and which other South American country?

13. Why is Bikini Atoll in the Marshall islands off-limits to visitors?
    A) Locals have objected to people wearing skimpy beach clothes
    B) It's home to a colony of rare wandering albatrosses
    C) It was the site of numerous nuclear tests in the 1940s and 50s.

14. What is the name of this famous Venetian bridge?

15. Over how many days is the annual Coachella music festival held?
    A) Two B) Four C) Six

16. The largest stone pyramid ever built is which country?
    A) Egypt B) Sudan C) Mexico

17. What sort of tree features on the flag of Lebanon?
    A) Cedar B) Sycamore C) Oak

18. New Caledonia is a Pacific territory of which European country?

19. A German speciality, rollmops is what type of pickled fish rolled around a savoury filling?
    A) Shark B) Cod C) Herring

20. The tiny island group of Tristan da Cunha, which has a population of about 250 people, is usually cited as the most remote inhabited place on Earth, lying over 2780km (1730 miles) from the nearest country. For three points, in what ocean would you find it, what is that nearest country, and to what country does the island group belong?

Quiz 17 **South Africa**

1. How many capital cities does South Africa have?
    A) One B) Two C) Three

2. What is the correct name for the wildlife park located in the northeast of the country?
    A) Luger B) Kruger C) Booger

3. What is a potjiekos?
    A) A traditional dance
    B) A traditional dish
    C) A traditional weapon

4. How many official languages does South Africa have?
    A) One B) Five C) Eleven

5. What is the most commonly spoken language in South Africa?
    A) English B) Afrikaans C) Zulu

6. The country's largest mountain range is the Drakensberg.
    What does Drakensberg mean in Afrikaans?
    A) Dragon Mountain B) Giant Mountain C) Male Duck Mountain

7. What is name for the strip of sea between two offshore islands where great white sharks are regularly sighted?
    A) Shark Avenue B) Shark Alley C) Shark Boulevard

8. How many colours are there on the South African flag?
    A) Four B) Five C) Six

9. Which South African city is home to what has been called the world's 'largest urban, human-made forest'?

10. The town of Franschhoek is particularly associated with what form of agriculture?
    A) Wine making B) Sheep farming C) Citrus orchards

11. On which ocean does the port city of Durban lie?

12. What was the name of the archbishop who oversaw South Africa's Truth and Reconciliation Commission following the abolition of Apartheid in the 1990s?

13. A popular tourist attraction in Cape Town, what is Kirstenbosch?
    A) A museum of African history
    B) The country's oldest cricket stadium
    C) A national botanical garden

14. What is the name of this famous natural landmark?

15. South Africa is responsible for 80% of the global production of which precious metal?

16. Which of these animals cannot be found living in the wild in South Africa
    A) Lions B) Tigers C) Elephants B) Ostriches C) Penguins

17. What is the name of the South African plant used to make a distinctive red-coloured herbal tea?
    A) Chamomile B) Camellia sinensis C) Rooibos

18. What is the longest river in South Africa?
    A) Blue River B) Orange River C) Limpopo River

19. Can you name the South African author who in 1999 became the first person to win the Booker prize for literature a second time?

20. Can you name the six countries that have land borders with South Africa? You get a point for each.

   Score

Quiz 18 **Train Travel**

1. In what country would you find the world's highest railway line and railway station?
   A) China B) Peru C) Switzerland

2. Built by George Stephenson, what was the name of the locomotive that in 1829 won the competition to run on England's Liverpool–Manchester line, the world's first inter-city train service?
   A) *Puffing Billy* B) *Rocket* C) *Starship*

3. The two main cities served by the luxurious train service the Orient Express were Paris in Europe and where in Asia?

4. The Rocky Mountaineer is a scenic train service in which country?
   A) Australia B) Peru C) Canada

5. In what decade of the 20th century did Japan's famous *Shinkansen*, or bullet trains, begin operating?
   A) 1930s B) 1960s C) 1980s

6. How long is the main route between Moscow and Vladivostok of the Trans-Siberian Railway, the world's longest railway?
   A) 5289km (3286 miles)
   B) 7289km (4529 miles)
   C) 9289km (5772 miles)

7. The world's fastest passenger trains operate in which country?
   A) USA B) France C) China

8. The British train *Mallard* holds what claim to fame?
   A) It set the world-speed record for a steam train
   B) It was the first train to travel the full width of the USA
   C) It can travel both on land and underwater

9. Which country has the world's longest railway network?
   A) USA B) Germany C) China

10. What US city's elevated train service is know as the 'L'?

11. Stretching over 7.3km (4.5 miles) and with 682 wagons loaded with iron ore, the longest ever train ran through which country in 2001?
A) Mauritania B) Australia C) Brazil

12. What is the name of the luxurious train service that travels between Pretoria and Cape Town in South Africa?
A) The Orange Train B) The Green Train C) The Blue Train

13. Used by an average of over 3.5 million people per day, in which city would you find the world's busiest train station?
A) Tokyo, Japan B) New York, USA C) Cairo, Egypt

14. The world's most southerly train service is a heritage line at the southern tip of Argentina known as 'The Train at the end of the World', but what was its original purpose when opened in 1909?
A) Carrying supplies to the local prison
B) Carrying equipment for researchers heading to Antarctica
C) Transporting glacier ice to local cities

15. What city's metro (local transit) train system is the largest in the world, in terms of its number of stations?
A) London, England B) Delhi, India C) New York, USA

16. If you're travelling aboard the Indian-Pacific train service, what country are you crossing?

17. The world's first underground train service opened in London in what year?
A) 1833 B) 1863 C) 1893

18. Just over twenty years later, the world's second underground train service opened in what city?
A) New York, USA B) Paris, France C) Budapest, Hungary

19. In what film do Marilyn Monroe, Jack Lemmon and Tony Curtis travel by train from Chicago to Miami?

20. Introduced in 1862, the *Flying Scotsman* is an express passenger train service that operates between which two British cities?

Quiz 19 **Central America**

1. Bordered by Mexico to the north and Colombia to the south, how many countries are there in Central America?

2. What is the geographical term for the long thin strip of land that makes up Central America, and which links North America with South America?
    A) Archipelago B) Peninsula C) Isthmus

3. What is the name of this popular dive site off the coast of Belize?
    A) The Blue Hole B) Challenger Deep C) The Java Trench

4. Who were the people that built the ancient ceremonial cities of Tikal in Guatemala and Caracol in Belize, among others?

5. Costa Rica's Isla del Coco formed the basis for the fictional 'Isla Nublar' in what blockbuster film series?
    A) Jurassic Park B) The Lord of the Rings C) Avengers

6. What is Central America's only volcano-less country?
    A) El Salvador B) Panama C) Belize

7. The longest road in the world, the Pan American Highway stretches for almost 30,000km (19,000 miles) from the tip of North America to the bottom of South America, except for a 96km (60 mile) gap in which Central American country?

8. *Gallo pinto*, the national dish of Costa Rica, consists of what?
    A) Fried chicken B) Rice and beans C) Pork stew

9. In 2021, El Salvador became the first country to make what legal tender?

10. Which country built the Panama Canal and controlled it until 1979?
    A) Colombia B) USA C) France

11. How long is the Panama Canal?
    A) 82km (51m) B) 182km (113 miles) C) 882km (548 miles)

12. Guatemala's currency is named after which colourful bird?
    A) Toucan B) Macaw C) Quetzal

13. Which of these statements about Belize is correct?
    A) Its capital is called Belize City
    B) Its seas are home to the world's second largest barrier reef
    C) Its national motto is 'Belize and thank you'

14. What is the capital of Costa Rica?
    A) San José B) Tegucigalpa C) Caracas

15. *Tortuga verde* is the Spanish name of which aquatic creature that nests on Costa Rica's beaches?

16. Lake Nicaragua is the only freshwater lake that's also home to what?
    A) Whales B) Sharks C) Squid

17. At 4203m (13,789ft), Volcán Tajumulco is the tallest mountain in Central America. In what country would you find it?
    A) Honduras B) Nicaragua C) Guatemala

18. What big cat has a range that encompasses 28 countries from Canada through Central America down to the southern tip of Chile?
    A) Jaguar B) Puma C) Ocelot

19. A traditional Guatemalan gift for children, what are *muñecas quitapenas*?
    A) Dolls B) Juggling balls C) Braided skipping ropes

20. By area, what is the largest country in Central America?

Quiz 20 **Museums and Galleries**

1. Perhaps the world's most famous picture, the *Mona Lisa* by Leonardo da Vinci can be seen in which art museum?

2. What is the name of this picture by the Dutch painter Rembrandt around which people are gathered in Amsterdam's Rijksmuseum?

3. In 1929, Abby Rockefeller, the wife of the financier John D. Rockefeller Jr, established MoMA in New York. What does MoMA stand for?

4. In what country could you visit Mona, the Museum of Old and New Art?
   A) Australia B) New Zealand C) South Africa

5. In what city was the world's first public museum opened in 1683?
   A) Oxford, England B) Athens, Greece C) Beijing, China

6. Founded in 1471, but not opened to the public till 1734, in what city would you find the world's oldest museum?
   A) Edinburgh, Scotland B) Rome, Italy C) Istanbul, Turkey

7. Which of the following is not a real museum?
   A) The Beijing Tap Water Museum, China
   B) The Dog Collar Museum, Kent, England
   C) The Museum of High-Heeled Shoes, Milan, Italy

8. What is the jokey nickname of the Siriraj Medical Museum in Bangkok, Thailand?
   A) Museum of Life B) Museum of Death C) Museum of Blood

9. Sir John Soane's Museum in London, England, displays a series of eight paintings known as *A Rake's Progress* by which satirical artist?
A) James Gillray B) Honré Daumier C) William Hogarth

10. What is the full name of the New York Museum usually known as 'The Met'?

11. The Frietmuseum in Bruges, Belgium is dedicated to what?
A) Potato fries B) Fridge freezers C) Fridays

12. Which part of the great scientist Galileo Galilei can you see on display in Museo Galileo in Florence, Italy?
A) His right eye B) His middle finger C) His ear

13. In what city would you find South Africa's National Gallery?

14. Which South American capital city has a museum dedicated to gold (*El Museo de Oro*)?

15. The painting *Christ of Saint John of the Cross* in the Kelvingrove Art Gallery, Glasgow, Scotland, is by which Spanish artist?
A) Pablo Picasso B) Salvador Dalí C) Diego Velázquez

16. The Kunstkamera, Russia's first museum, which opened in 1727, was established by which ruler?

17. Profits from the Great Exhibition in 1851 helped establish which three museums in London, England?

18. The China Science and Technology Museum is in which city?
A) Beijing B) Shanghai C) Guangzhou

19. The Bata Museum in Toronto, Canada, is given over entirely to displays of which item of clothing?
A) Hats B) Gloves C) Shoes

20. In which English city can you visit the National Football Museum?
A) Liverpool B) Manchester C) London

Quiz 21 **Around the World in 25 Capitals**

1. By population, what is the world's largest capital city?
    A) Tokyo, Japan B) Mexico City, Mexico C) Dhaka, Bangladesh

2. And what is the world's smallest capital city?
    A) Valletta, Malta B) Vatican City C) Ngerulmud, Palau

3. What was the first capital of the Roman province of Britannia?
    A) Londinium (London)
    B) Camulodunum (Colchester)
    C) Eboracum (York)

4. What is the capital of Colombia?

5. Dakar is the capital city of which African country?

6. Vientiane is the capital of which Southeast Asian country?

7. This monument lies at the heart of which capital city? And for
    a bonus point what is the name of the monument?

8. In what decade of the 20th century did Canberra become capital
    of Australia?

9. Ulaanbaatar is the capital of which Asian country?

10. What is the capital of Cameroon?

11. Suva is the capital of which Pacific island nation?

12. What is the name of the river on which both Montevideo, the capital of Uruguay, and Buenos Aires, the capital of Argentina, lie?
    A) Orinoco B) Paraná C) Río de la Plata

13. Baron Haussmann undertook a massive rebuilding programme of which European capital in the 19th century?
    A) Vienna, Austria B) Paris, France C) Berlin, Germany

14. The architect Oscar Niemeyer is perhaps best known for designing which purpose-built capital city in the 1950s?
    A) Islamabad, Pakistan B) Brasilia, Brazil C) Gaborone, Botswana

15. The Rijksmuseum is a major art museum in which European capital city?

16. Port of Spain is the capital of which Caribbean country?

17. What is the capital of the Czech Republic?

18. The capital of the Seychelles is named after which British Queen?
    A) Boudica B) Elizabeth C) Victoria

19. What is the capital of North Korea?

20. Dili is the capital of which Southeast Asian country?

21. What was the capital of the USA immediately before the adoption of Washington DC in 1800?
    A) Boston B) Philadelphia C) New York

22. In which Asian capital city would you find the Forbidden City?

23. Abuja replaced which city as the capital of Nigeria in 1991?

24. Paramaribo is the capital of which South American country?

25. The city of Budapest was created in 1873 following the merger of two separate cities, Buda and Pest. True or false?

Quiz 22 **South America**

1. Colombia is the world's largest producer of which gemstones?
   A) Rubies B) Emeralds C) Diamonds

2. What three countries share a border with Paraguay?
   A) Bolivia, Brazil and Argentina
   B) Bolivia, Brazil and Uruguay
   C) Bolivia, Chile and Argentina

3. Native to South America, what is the world's largest snake?
   A) King cobra B) Black mamba C) Green anaconda

4. Located in Peru's Nazca Desert, what are the 'Nazca Lines'?
   A) A Formula 1 race track
   B) Giant ancient drawings etched on the desert floor
   C) Very long, thin sand dunes

5. What is *salteña*, the national dish of Bolivia?
   A) A baked empanada filled with stew
   B) A fried tortilla filled with beans
   C) A salt-baked river fish

6. The Corcovado Rack Railway takes visitors up to see which South American attraction?
   A) The Christ the Redeemer statue, Rio de Janeiro, Brazil
   B) Machu Picchu, Peru
   C) Angel Falls, Venezuela

7. Which country used to be known as Dutch Guiana?
   A) Guyana B) Suriname C) Venezuela

8. Famed for its giant carved stone heads, Rapa Nui, also known as Easter Island, is a territory of which South American country?
   A) Chile B) Ecuador C) Peru

9. *Chivas* are buses serving Colombia's rural areas. What is a *chiva*?
   A) A goat B) A jaguar C) A piranha

10. A popular dish in Chile, what is *carbonada*?
    A) A pasta dish with bacon and eggs
    B) A vegetable and meat stew
    C) A vegetable frittata topped with plantain

11. Which South American country is one of the world's biggest exporters of cut flowers?
    A) Colombia B) Peru C) Argentina

12. What features in the top left-hand corner of Uruguay's flag?
    A) A llama B) The Sun C) A bird

13. What is the currency of Venezuela?
    A) Venezuelan peso B) Venezuelan dollar C) Venezuelan bolivar

14. What is the largest city in Chile?
    A) Antofagasta B) Valparaíso C) Santiago

15. The potato is native to the Peruvian-Bolivian Andes. How many varieties of potato are grown in Peru?
    A) Around 400 B) Around 1400 C) Around 4000

16. Peru's executive capital La Paz is home to the world's highest what?
    A) Statue B) Cable car system C) Airport

17. Uruguay's football team has won the FIFA World Cup twice. In which years?
    A) 1930 and 1950 B) 1938 and 1950 C) 1950 and 1970

18. What is the official language of Guyana?
    A) Spanish B) Portuguese C) English

19. Bolivia's Salar de Uyuni is the world's biggest what?
    A) Solar power plant B) Salt flat C) Sand dune

20. In 2011, Paraguay's cooks created a world record-breaking what to celebrate the country's 200 years of independence?
    A) Cake B) Hot dog C) Loaf

Quiz 23 **Japan**

1. By what name was the city of Tokyo known before 1868, the year it became Japan's capital?
    A) Kyoto B) Edo C) Yokohama

2. Each spring, the Japanese Meteorological Agency releases a forecast to help citizens plan for *hanami*. What does this forecast relate to?
    A) The rainy season B) Snow storms C) Cherry blossom

3. Who is the head of state in Japan?
    A) The emperor B) The king C) The president

4. Tokyo's train lines employ people known as *oshiya* during rush hour. What do *oshiya* do?
    A) Make sure passengers keep their feet off seats
    B) Push passengers onto packed trains
    C) Sell snacks and beverages from portable vending machines

5. What is unusual about the Henn-Na Hotel, which opened in Nagasaki in 2015?
    A) Half of the rooms are underwater
    B) It has paper walls
    C) It is partially staffed by robots

6. Shibuya Crossing in Tokyo is believed to be the busiest pedestrian crossing in the world. On average, how many people cross the intersection every time the lights change?
    A) 500 B) 1500 C) 2500

7. The Hachiko statue is a popular meeting point outside Shibuya station. What sort of animal was Hachiko?
    A) A bear B) A dog C) A crane

8. How many main islands make up the country of Japan?
    A) Two B) Three C) Four

9. In total, how many islands does Japan have?
    A) Around 70 B) Around 700 C) Around 7000

10. By population, what is Japan's second largest city?
    A) Osaka B) Yokohama C) Kyoto

11. The district of Akihabara in Tokyo is the place to go if you want
    to shop for what?
    A) Sushi B) Traditional clothing C) Anime and manga

12. A *ryokan* is a traditional Japanese what?
    A) Inn B) Song C) Hat

13. In 2021, Tokyo hosted the postponed 2020 Summer Olympics.
    In what previous year had the city staged the games?
    A) 1952 B) 1964 C) 1972

14. Athletes taking part in the 2020 Olympic games slept on beds
    made out of recycled what?
    A) Cardboard B) Plastic C) Glass

15. Mitaka, a city in the western region of Greater Tokyo, is home to a
    museum dedicated to the work of what Japanese animation studio?

16. What is the name of the Japanese dish made of meat, seafood
    or vegetables that have been battered and deep fried?

17. Jigokudani Monkey Park in Nagano Prefecture, is famous for
    its population of hot-spring-loving primates. What kind of
    monkey are they?
    A) Marmosets B) Macaques C) Gibbons

18. What is the national sport of Japan?
    A) Basketball C) Kendo C) Sumo

19. One of the largest markets in the world, Tokyo's Toyosu Market
    specialises in what?
    A) Fish and seafood B) Furniture C) Flowers

20. The ancient city of Kyoto is home to a particularly high
    concentration of buildings known as *machiya*. What are *machiya*?
    A) Skyscrapers B) Wooden townhouses C) Capsule hotels

Quiz 24 **Forests and Jungles**

1. Home to around a third of Earth's known species, what is the largest tropical rainforest on the planet?
    A) The Amazon B) The Congo C) The Daintree Rainforest

2. And what is the second largest?
    A) The Amazon B) The Congo C) The Daintree Rainforest

3. The Bwindi Impenetrable Forest located in south-western Uganda is home to almost half of the world's population of what?
    A) Black rhinos B) African wild dogs C) Mountain gorillas

4. The Firhmin Forest of Socotra, off the coast of Yemen, is home to which fantastically named species of tree?
    A) Dragon's blood tree B) Wolf's bane tree C) Fairy wing tree

5. The Amazon Rainforest spans Brazil, Bolivia, Ecuador, Venezuela, Guyana, Suriname and which two other countries?
    A) Peru, Colombia B) Guyana, Chile C) Argentina, Uruguay

6. The forests of which island provide a home to almost all of the world's species of tree kangaroo?
    A) New Guinea B) Borneo C) Java

7. Which islands are the only places in the world where elephants, rhinos, orangutans and tigers live side by side?
    A) Borneo, Sumatra B) Madagascar, Mauritius C) Komodo, Rinca

8. What is the name given to the great stretches of coniferous forest forming a belt around the subarctic region of the world.
    A) Sylvan B) Taiga C) Wald

9. The Daintree Rainforest, believed to be world's oldest rainforest, is in which country?
    A) Peru B) Indonesia C) Australia

10. The Japanese city of Kyoto boasts a forest of what?
    A) Cherry trees B) Oak trees C) Bamboo

11. With about 75% of its land covered in trees, what is Europe's most forested country?
A) Germany B) Finland C) France

12. What's the name of the huge mangrove forest that stretches across parts of coastal India and Bangladesh?
A) Sunda Shelf B) Sundarbans C) Indochina mangroves

13. Just outside San Francisco, California, Muir Woods National Monument is known for its forest of what?
A) Oaks B) Maples C) Redwoods

14. Also in California, what's special about a bristlecone pine named Methuselah?
A) It's one of the oldest trees in the world
B) It's one of the tallest trees in the world
C) It's one of the widest trees in the world

15. Can you identify this famous forest from the following description? A large forested mountain range in south-west Germany, its name comes from the thick, dark pine woods that flourish there.

16. What is the Japanese tree-themed activity called *shinrin yoku*?
A) Tree climbing B) Den building C) Forest bathing

17. What type of Australian tree is also known as a gum tree?
A) Acacia B) Eucalyptus C) Banksia

18. The pillar-like rock formations in Zhangjiajie National Forest Park, China, inspired the alien landscapes of which sci-fi film?
A) *Revenge of the Sith* B) *Avatar* C) *Dune*

19. Home to sea otters, forests made of what grow off the west coast of North America?
A) Kelp B) Sea grass C) Plankton

20. Found in the cloud forests of the Andes, what is South America's only native species of bear?
A) The sun bear B) The sloth bear C) The spectacled bear

Quiz 25 **Planes and Air Travel**

1. What were the first names of the American Wright Brothers who made the world's first successful powered flight?

2. In what year did their historic first flight take place?
    A) 1893 B) 1903 C) 1913

3. In what year was the world's first commercial passenger flight?
    A) 1914 B) 1924 C) 1934

4. Who was the first person to fly solo across the English Channel?
    A) Louis Blériot B) Charles Lindbergh C) Howard Hughes

5. What country has the highest number of airports, at over 13,500?
    A) USA B) China C) Russia

6. What is the typical height at which commercial airliners fly?
    A) 26,000ft (8000m)
    B) 36,000ft (10,000m)
    C) 46,000ft (14,000m)

7. The world's longest direct commercial flight currently runs between New York and Singapore. How long does it last?
    A) 12 hours, 50 minutes
    B) 18 hours, 50 minutes
    C) 22 hours, 50 minutes

8. Which of these statements is correct?
    A) It's generally quicker to fly from the USA to the UK
    B) It's generally quicker to fly from the UK to the USA
    C) Both flights generally take the same amount of time

9. Founded in 1919, KLM is the world's oldest airline. Of which country is it the national carrier?
    A) Kenya B) South Korea C) The Netherlands

10. What is the nickname of the Boeing 747 airliner?

11. Concorde, the world's only supersonic aircraft, which operated from 1976 to 2003, was a collaboration between which two countries?

12. What's unusual about Japan's Kansai Airport?
    A) It's over 500km (300 miles) from its hub city
    B) It's been built on an artificial island
    C) It only serves propeller-powered planes

13. In which country would you find an airport named after James Bond author Ian Fleming?
    A) UK B) USA C) Jamaica

14. At the end of the movie *Casablanca*, where does Ingrid Bergman's character catch a plane to?
    A) London B) Lisbon C) Paris

15. Which of these airports is the farthest north you can fly to on a commercial plane?
    A) John O'Groats Airport, Scotland
    B) Resolute Bay Airport, Canada
    C) Svalbard Airport, Norway

16. In the 1980s, American Airlines saved $40,000 a year by removing one what from each meal served in first class?
    A) Olive from the salad
    B) Spoon from the cutlery set
    C) Serving of butter

17. Who was the first woman to fly solo from the UK to Australia?
    A) Amelia Earthart B) Bessie Coleman C) Amy Johnson

18. Which country has an airport named after Mother Teresa?
    A) India B) Turkey C) Albania

19. Singapore Changi Airport has the world's tallest what?
    A) Indoor waterfall C) Air traffic control tower C) Terminal

20. In what country is the airline Qantas based?

Quiz 26 **General Travel Knowledge**

1. According to legend, the order of the animals representing the Chinese signs of the Zodiac was decided by a what?
   A) A race B) A fight C) A battle of wits

2. 'Empire State of Mind' by Jay-Z and Alicia Keys is a song about which US city?

3. Which award-winning Colombian author, often known affectionately as 'Gabo', wrote the Colombia-set novel, *Love in the Time of Cholera*?

4. The walls and moat surrounding Bourtange Fortress in the Netherlands famously form what shape?
   A) A star B) A cross C) A triangle

5. What is the name of the fermented flatbread widely eaten in Ethiopia and Eritrea?
   A) Injera B) Wat C) Teff

6. Purim is a holiday in which religion?
   A) Sikhism B) Islam C) Judaism

7. Which of these Australian mammals is not a marsupial?
   A) Hairy-footed dunnart
   B) Long-nosed potoroo
   C) Short-beaked echidna

8. What is the shallowest ocean?
   A) Arctic B) Southern C) Indian

9. What is the world's second largest island
   A) New Guinea B) Borneo C) Madagascar

10. What once-endangered creature is the national animal of Jordan, Oman, Qatar and the United Arab Emirates?
    A) The Arabian leopard B) The Arabian oryx C) The Arabian wolf

11. In what year was the Tour de France first held?
    A) 1853 B) 1903 C) 1953

12. In what East African country would you find the port city
    of Mombasa?
    A) Kenya B) Tanzania C) Mozambique

13. Found living on the coastlines of southern Australia and New
    Zealand, what is the world's smallest species of penguin?
    A) The little penguin
    B) The pygmy penguin
    C) The tiny penguin

14. The Statue of Liberty stands on which island in New York Harbor?
    A) Coney Island B) Liberty Island C) Long Island

15. Edson Arantes do Nascimento is the real full name of which
    iconic footballer?

16. Ogopogo is a dinosaur-like monster said to inhabit a lake in
    which country?
    A) Scotland B) Canada C) Uruguay

17. What are the decorated sugar skulls eaten during Mexico's Day
    of the Dead celebrations called?
    A) *Calaveras* B) *Pozoles* C) *Tostadas*

18. The Azadi Tower is a major monument in which Middle Eastern
    capital city?
    A) Baghdad, Iraq B) Beirut, Lebanon C) Tehran, Iran

19. In the mid 20th century, a 1833km (1139 mile) fence, the longest
    in the world, was completed across Western Australia to protect
    against the unchecked spread of which invasive species?
    A) Foxes B) Rabbits C) Dingoes

20. Where is the headquarters of the WTO (World Trade Organization)?
    A) Geneva, Switzerland B) Washington DC, USA C) Beijing, China

Quiz 27 **Egypt**

1. What is the capital of Egypt?

2. The longest river in the world, the Nile runs through 11 African countries, eventually reaching the sea in Egypt. How long is it?
   A) 5650km (3510 mi) B) 6650km (4100 mi) C) 7650km (4750 mi)

3. What is the popular Egyptian dish made from a combination of rice, lentils, pasta, chickpeas, tomato sauce and crispy onions called?
   A) Kofta B) Kebab C) Koshari

4. What is the national drink of Egypt?
   A) Tea B) Coffee C) Ginger beer

5. How many UNESCO world heritage sites are located in Egypt?
   A) Four B) Seven C) Eleven

6. What is the name of the ancient Egyptian jackal-headed god of mummification, shown below?
   A) Ra B) Osiris C) Anubis

7. The three giant pyramids at Giza were originally built as what?
   A) Palaces B) Tombs C) Temples

8. The holiday resort of Sharm El-Sheikh is located on which sea?
   A) The Black Sea B) The Mediterranean Sea C) The Red Sea

9. The Egyptian flag features which three main colours?
   A) Red, white, blue B) Red, white, black C) Red, green, black

10. What is the name of the area outside the ancient city of Thebes where, for a period of around 500 years, the Egyptians buried their pharaohs and powerful nobles in rock-cut tombs?

11. The mortuary temple of which female pharaoh is located at Deir el-Bahri, also in Thebes?
A) Hatshepsut B) Nefertiti C) Cleopatra

12. What pharaoh's tomb was discovered more or less intact by the British archaeologist Howard Carter in 1922?

13. What is the official currency of Egypt?
A) Egyptian dollar B) Egyptian pound C) Egyptian dinar

14. Once found throughout the Nile Delta, and used by the ancient Egyptians to make paper, which plant is now quite rare in Egypt?
A) Lotus B) Date palm C) Papyrus

15. Approximately how much of Egypt is covered in desert?
A) 30% B) 50% C) 90%

16. Connecting the Mediterranean Sea to the Red Sea through Egypt, the Suez Canal opened in what decade?
A) 1860s B) 1890s C) 1920s

17. Of the original Seven Wonders of the Ancient World, two were in Egypt. The Great Pyramid was one. What was the other?

18. In the 1960s, the ancient temple of Abu Simbel had to be relocated due to the construction of what?
A) Aswan High Dam B) Cairo Airport C) Suez Canal extension

19. Which pharaoh of the 13th century BCE is known for having built many colossal statues of himself?
A) Thutmose I B) Ramses II C) Amenhotep III

20. What is the name of the object, discovered in 1799, that allowed scholars to finally decipher Egyptian hieroglyphs?

Quiz 28 **Pacific Islands**

1. Which Pacific country is the world's smallest island nation?
   A) Palau B) Nauru C) Vanuatu

2. What is considered the national sport of Fiji?
   A) Rugby union B) Surfing C) Baseball

3. Can you name the trickster who appears in folk tales throughout Polynesia? He gave fire to the people in Samoan mythology and drew up the islands from the deep in Tongan mythology.
   A) Anansi B) Maui C) Loki

4. An *'ie tōga* is a highly valued item in Samoa, often presented as a gift at weddings, funerals and other special occasions. What is it?
   A) A necklace B) A finely woven mat C) A drinking vessel

5. Which animals travel nearly 5,000km (3,000 miles) every year to breeding grounds off the coast of Tonga?
   A) Green turtles B) Humpback whales C) Bottlenose dolphins

6. There are nine stars on the flag of Tuvalu. What do they represent?
   A) The nine islands that make up Tuvalu
   B) The nation's nine original founders
   C) The nine main stars of the Carina constellation

7. Which future US president was saved by Solomon Islanders when he was marooned on an uninhabited island during World War II?
   A) Ronald Reagan B) John F Kennedy C) Richard Nixon

8. Which of these statements about Kiribati is not true?
   A) Lying deep in the Pacific, it was only discovered in 1979
   B) It is the only nation to straddle all four hemispheres
   C) It is the first territory to welcome the New Year

9. Many of the islands in the Pacific are atolls. What is an atoll?
   A) A ring-shaped coral island encircling a lagoon
   B) A long thin coral island that tapers down to a point
   C) A group of three coral islands forming a triangle shape

10. Which extreme sport is believed to have its origins in the 'land diving' ritual performed on Pentecost Island in Vanuatu?
    A) Sky diving B) Hang gliding C) Bungee jumping

11. Approximately how many islands make up the nation of Fiji?
    A) 100 B) 200 C) 300

12. On what side of the road do people drive in Samoa?

13. What is the name of the flower necklaces given as gifts across Polynesia to symbolise peace and friendship?
    A) Heis B) Leis C) Keis

14. The giant bats known as flying foxes, which live on many Pacific islands, including Tonga, feed mainly on what?
    A) Blood B) Fruit C) Rats

15. Many French Polynesian homes used to have homemade metal 'mailboxes' for taking delivery, not of letters, but of what?
    A) Flowers B) Milk C) Bread

16. For a brief period in the 20th century, Nauru was the world's richest nation. What was that wealth based on?
    A) Gold deposits B) Guano deposits C) Tuna fishing

17. In what Pacific country would you find the ruins of the medieval city of Nan Madol?
    A) Solomon Islands B) Tuvalu C) Federated States of Micronesia

18. What are *rai*, which were once used as currency on Yap island?
    A) Cowrie shells B) Giant stone discs C) Lobster claws

19. The island of Fakarava in French Polynesia is home to a church made entirely from what?
    A) Coral B) Coconut shells C) Driftwood

20. Found on many islands across the Pacific, what is the world's largest land invertebrate?
    A) Coconut crab B) Pacific Island spider C) Giant millipede

Quiz 29 **Languages**

1. Roughly, how many languages are spoken in the world today?
    A) 1000 B) 4000 C) 7000

2. Most of the world speaks one of 20 languages. As of 2022, what is the most spoken language in the world?
    A) Mandarin B) English C) Hindi

3. And where does Spanish rank in the list of top 20 languages?
    A) Fourth B) Tenth C) Twentieth

4. What percentage of the world's languages are at risk of dying out?
    A) 25% B) 40% C) 65%

5. What is the world's most linguistically diverse country with over 800 languages?
    A) Nigeria B) USA C) Papua New Guinea

6. In what context would you use the Sanskrit word *namaste*?
    A) To greet someone
    B) To apologise to someone
    C) To ask for directions

7. Which French classic is the second most translated book in the world after the Bible?
    A) *Les Misérables* by Victor Hugo
    B) *Madame Bovary* by Gustave Flaubert
    C) *The Little Prince* by Antoine de Saint-Exupéry

8. The Walt Disney film *The Lion King* made the phrase *hakuna matata* ('no worries') world famous, but what African language does it come from?
    A) Somali B) Swahili C) Amharic

9. What is the official language of Brazil?

10. How many official languages are recognised in India?
    A) One B) Two C) Twenty-two

11. What is the official language of the USA?
    A) English B) Spanish C) It doesn't have one

12. Following immigration from Europe in the 19th century, which South American country has a collection of (partly) Welsh-speaking villages?
    A) Colombia B) Brazil C) Argentina

13. What does the Italian word *prego* mean?
    A) Hello B) Thank you C) You're welcome

14. Which language has the longest alphabet with 74 letters?
    A) Swedish B) Khmer (Cambodian) C) Greek

15. Roughly, how many different types of sign language are used in the world today?
    A) 100 B) 200 C) 300

16. The English words 'cookie', 'cruise' and 'yacht' derive from which European language?
    A) French B) German C) Dutch

17. Arabic is the third most popular official language in the world. How many countries have it as an official language?
    A) 15 B) 27 C) 32

18. What do *ursäkta* in Swedish, *sumimasen* in Japanese and *pardon* in French all mean?
    A) Hello B) Excuse me C) See you later

19. What are the two main languages spoken on board the International Space Station?
    A) English and Mandarin
    B) English and Spanish
    C) English and Russian

20. If you were driving along a German motoryway and saw a sign saying *Ausfahrt* what would you expect to see coming up?
    A) An exit B) A roundabout C) A mountain

Quiz 30 **World Landmarks**

Can you name the landmark from the three options available?

1. A) The Louvre, France
   B) The Lincoln Memorial, USA
   C) The Parthenon, Greece

2. A) Christ the Redeemer, Brazil
   B) Christ of the Ozarks, USA
   C) Christ the King, Poland

3. A) Marble Arch, UK
   B) Arch of Constantine, Rome
   C) Arc de Triomphe, France

4. A) The Eiffel Tower, France
   B) The Tokyo Tower, Japan
   C) Nelson's Column, UK

5. A) Sydney Opera House, Australia
   B) Lotus Temple, Delhi
   C) Guggenheim Museum, Spain

6. A) Great Mosque of Algiers, Algeria
   B) Grand Mosque of Paris, France
   C) Great Mosque of Djenné, Mali

7. A) Q1 Tower, Australia
   B) The Shard, UK
   C) Shanghai Tower, China

8. A) Sky Tower, New Zealand
    B) Space Needle, USA
    C) CN Tower, Canada

9. A) One World Trade Center, USA
    B) The Gherkin, UK
    C) Gran Torre Santiago, Chile

10. A) St Paul's Cathedral, UK
    B) St Peter's Basilica, Italy
    C) Sacré-Coeur, France

11. A) Florence Cathedral, Italy
    B) Hagia Sophia, Turkey
    C) Angkor Wat, Cambodia

12. A) Cathedral of Brasília, Brazil
    B) L'Oceanogràfic, Spain
    C) Sydney Opera House, Australia

13. A) The Colosseum, Italy
    B) The Alamo, USA
    C) Great Zimbabwe, Zimbabwe

14. A) Neuschwanstein, Germany
    B) Disneyland, USA
    C) St Basil's Cathedral, Russia

15. A) Kings Prism Tower, Kenya
    B) Bank of China Tower, China
    C) Petronas Towers, Malaysia

Quiz 31 **General Travel Knowledge**

1. The Blue Mosque, also known as the Sultan Ahmet Mosque, is a 17th-century religious building in which country?
    A) Iran B) Turkey C) Azerbaijan

2. In what year was the Roman city of Pompeii destroyed by an erupting Mount Vesuvius?
    A) 30 BCE B) 79 CE C) 125 CE

3. What is the capital of Bangladesh?

4. From which country did Papua New Guinea gain independence in 1975?
    A) France B) UK C) Australia

5. The singer Elvis Presley was born in which US state in 1935?
    A) Tennessee B) Louisiana C) Mississippi

6. Which Central American country abolished its army in 1949? It remains one of the few countries without a standing military force.
    A) Panama B) Costa Rica C) Nicaragua

7. According to legend, the country of Moldova is named after what?
    A) A dog B) A vineyard C) A saint

8. Which Indian city is known as the pink city owing to all the buildings within its historic centre having been painted the same shade of terracotta?
    A) Jaipur B) Chennai C) Kolkata

9. Which of these statements about the city of St David's in Wales is true?
    A) It is the UK's oldest city
    B) It is the UK's smallest city
    C) It is the UK's highest city

10. Haiti shares the Caribbean island of Hispaniola with what other country?

11. The Moroccan flag has a green star on a what colour background?
    A) White B) Red C) Blue

12. What is the name of the stone statues on the Pacific island of
    Rapa Nui, or Easter Island, 3500km (2200 miles) off Chile's coast?
    A) Moai B) Ahu C) Rapas

13. Which African country has the largest population of cheetahs?
    A) Kenya B) Namibia C) South Africa

14. Once a British colony, the Ellice Islands became which independent
    Pacific country in 1978?
    A) Tuvalu B) Kiribati C) Palau

15. What Australian state is this?

16. Which French author wrote *L'Etranger* (The Stranger)?

17. What is the correct Italian term for the type of pasta that's
    shaped like little bow ties (Clue: it's derived from the Italian
    word for butterflies).
    A) Rigatoni B) Linguini C) Farfalle

18. What nationality was the painter Pablo Picasso?

19. The Bering Strait separates which two countries?

20. In what Asian city is Merdeka 118, which at 679m (2227ft) is
    (as of 2022), the world's second-highest building?
    A) Shanghai, China B) Dubai, UAE C) Kuala Lumpur, Malaysia

Quiz 32 **Western Europe**

1. Which Western European nation is the world's second smallest, after the Vatican City?
   A) San Marino B) Andorra C) Monaco

2. Which Western European nation is the world's only remaining grand duchy?
   A) Luxembourg B) Liechtenstein C) Andorra

3. The River Liffey flows through which capital city?
   A) Berlin, Germany B) Brussels, Belgium C) Dublin, Ireland

4. A popular treat, *Poffertjes* are Dutch what?
   A) Pancakes B) Chocolates C) Ice cream cones

5. How many official languages are there in Switzerland?
   A) 4 B) 40 C) 400

6. What is the name of perhaps the best-known work by the Belgian surrealist René Magritte? It depicts a man in a suit, wearing a bowler hat, his face obscured by an apple.

7. After the Second World War, which city became the capital of West Germany?
   A) Cologne B) Bonn C) Frankfurt

8. What is Andorra's currency?
   A) The Andorran franc B) The Andorran peseta C) The euro

9. In which Western European capital city was the Hollywood actor Audrey Hepburn born?
   A) London, UK B) Amsterdam, Netherlands C) Brussels, Belgium

10. Can you name the eight countries that have borders with France on mainland Europe? You get a point for each.

11. Which controversial French delicacy is made from goose liver?

12. Which river flows through the Austrian capital, Vienna?
   A) The Danube B) The Rhine C) The Elbe

13. The Alps mountain range spreads across how many European countries?
   A) Seven B) Eight C) Nine

14. Why are Belgium, the Netherlands and Luxembourg known as the Low Countries?
   A) To symbolise their solidarity, 'Low' being a Dutch word meaning 'friendship'
   B) Because so much of their territory is at or below sea level
   C) Because they used to be territories in the empire of the Lows, a German royal family of the Middle Ages

15. By population, what is the second largest city in the Republic of Ireland?
   A) Cork B) Limerick C) Galway

16. Liechtenstein City is the capital of Liechtenstein. True or false?

17. Which Western European city hosted the 1920 Summer Olympic Games
   A) Paris, France B) Antwerp, Belgium C) Amsterdam, Netherlands

18. Which Austrian classical composer wrote 'The Blue Danube' and 'Die Fledermaus'?
   A) Richard Strauss B) Franz Schubert C) Johann Strauss II

19. In which country is Carlsberg beer made?
   A) Netherlands B) Belgium C) Denmark

20. CWL is the code for an international airport in which European city?
   A) Cadiz, Spain
   B) Cardiff, Wales
   C) Cork, Republic of Ireland

Quiz 33 **Religious Buildings**

1. The Srirangam Temple in Tamil Nadu, India, is the largest Hindu temple in the world. True or false?

2. The world's largest Christian church is in Africa, True or false?

3. Where is the world's the largest Sikh temple outside India?
    A) USA B) Egypt C) Australia

4. In what country would you find the largest synagogue in the world?
    A) USA B) Israel C) Hungary

5. In what country would you find the largest mosque in the world?
    A) Pakistan B) Saudi Arabia C) Indonesia

6. In what country would you find the world's largest stone statue of Buddha?
    A) China B) Taiwan C) Sri Lanka

7. Which great Renaissance painter was partly responsible for designing St Peter's Basilica in Rome, Italy?
    A) Leonardo da Vinci B) Michelangelo C) Raphael

8. The Cathedral of Zipaquirá in Cundinamarca, Colombia, is in which unusual location?
    A) On a cliff edge, 200m (650ft) above ground
    B) In a salt mine 200m (650ft) below ground

9. Siddhārtha Gautama achieved enlightenment, allowing him to become the Buddha, while sat under a what in India?
    A) Cliff ledge B) Fig tree C) Rain cloud

10. St Basil's Cathedral, Moscow, with its distinctive onion domes, was built by which ruler?
    A) Ivan the Terrible B) Peter the Great C) Catherine the Great

11. Where would you find the Temple of Heaven?
    A) India B) Japan C) China

12. How many churches are there in Antarctica?
    A) None B) One C) Eight

13. Ulm Minster in Ulm, Germany , holds what claim to fame?
    A) It's the oldest church in Europe
    B) It's the tallest church in the world
    C) It's a combined mosque, synagogue and church

14. The Dome of the Rock in Jerusalem is sacred to which two religions?

15. In what building has almost every English monarch been crowned?
    A) St Paul's Cathedral B) Westminster Abbey C) Liverpool Cathedral

16. The largest religious structure in the world, just how big an area
    does Angkor Wat in Cambodia cover?
    A) 63 hectares (156 acres) B) 163 hectares (400 acres)

17. When was the distinctive Gaudi-designed church known as the
    Sagrada Família in Barcelona, Spain, completed?
    A) 1910 B) 2010 C) It's still not complete

18. In what city would you find this futuristic looking cathedral?
    A) Miami, USA B) Brasília, Brazil C) Sydney, Australia

19. Paro Taktsang Buddhist monastery in Bhutan also goes by which
    animal-themed name?
    A) Tiger's Nest B) Snow Leopard's Retreat C) Yak's Sanctuary

20. The Hassan II Mosque is in which Moroccan city?
    A) Rabat B) Marrakesh C) Casablanca

Quiz 34 **The Amazon**

1. How many countries does the main course of the Amazon River flow through?
    A) One B) Three C) Five

2. Roughly how big is the Amazon Basin?
    A) As big as France
    B) As big as the 48 contiguous US states
    C) As big as the Sahara Desert

3. Most of the river, and most of the surrounding rainforest, is found in which country?

4. Approximately what percentage of the world's terrestrial plants and animals live in the Amazon?
    A) 10% B) 20% C) 30%

5. How long is the Amazon River?
    A) 5400km (3355 miles)
    B) 6400km (3975 miles)
    C) 7400km (4600 miles)

6. The largest river by volume in the world, the Amazon carries more water than the next seven rivers combined. True or false?

7. Which of these is not a genuine tributary of the Amazon River?
    A) Negro B) Madeira C) Atbara

8. What is the largest city on the Amazon's banks?
    A) Manaus B) Rio de Janeiro C) São Paulo

9. The Amazon River empties into what ocean?

10. At its greatest extent, roughly how wide is the river's mouth at the point it meets the ocean?
    A) 3km (2 miles) B) 32km (20 miles) C) 325km (200 miles)

11. What is the Amazon's largest predator?
    A) Green anaconda B) Black caiman C) Jaguar

12. The most dangerous animals in the Amazon are generally thought to be the green anaconda, the red-bellied piranha and what small, brightly-coloured creatures?

13. How many tribes are estimated to still live in the Amazon Rainforest, having little contact with the outside world?
    A) 200 B) 400 C) 600

14. What percentage of the Amazon Rainforest has been destroyed since 2000?
    A) 2% B) 4% C) 8%

15. Found in the depths of the forest, the Goliath birdeater is the world's largest spider. It can have a leg span of up to what?
    A) 10cm (4 inches) B) 20 cm (8 inches) C) 30cm (12 inches)

16. The idea for the e-commerce company Amazon came to its founder Jeff Bezos during a trip through the Amazon jungle in the mid 1990s, hence the name. True or false?

17. Which of these is not a genuine Amazon monkey?
    A) Golden-handed tamarin
    B) Orange-faced spider monkey
    C) Black howler monkey

18. When mature, what colour is the Amazon river dolphin?
    A) Pink B) Green C) Blue

19. Roughly, how many species of fish are there in the Amazon River?
    A) 300 B) 3000 C) 30,000

20. Is this more or less than the number of species found in the North Atlantic Ocean?

Quiz 35 **Australia**

1. Mainland Australia is divided up into six states and six territories. True or false?

2. How many main time zones are there in Australia?
A) Three B) Five C) Three and Five

3. What constellation is depicted on the Australian flag?

4. Which is the longest river in Australia?
A) Murray River B) Murrumbidgee River C) Darling River

5. The original design of Sydney Opera House was supposedly based on what fruit?
A) A banana B) An orange C) A pineapple

6. Which Aboriginal device is believed to be the world's oldest wind instrument?

7. Koalas feed almost exclusively on the leaves of what type of tree?

8. Which Australian opera singer had two dishes created in her honour by the noted French chef Auguste Escoffier? And, for two bonus points, what are those dishes?

9. What is the collective noun for a group of kangaroos?
A) A hop B) A mob C) A pouch

10. Believed to be the smallest trophy in international sports, the 10cm (4 inch) tall Ashes urn, competed for by England and Australia in a biennial cricket competition, contains what?
A) Six further trophies, each smaller than the last, representing the maximum score a batsman can achieve with a single stroke
B) The burnt remains of the bails from a match in 1882, in which Australia had beaten England for the first time on English soil
C) The burnt remains of the first ball bowled in an international match between England and Australia

11. In what territory or state is Uluru located?
    A) Western Australia B) South Australia C) Northern Territory

12. Which Australian auteur wrote and directed the films *Moulin Rouge* and *Strictly Ballroom*?

13. What is a pademelon?
    A) A desert oasis fed by an underground water source
    B) A small marsupial related to wallabies and kangaroos
    C) A large insect larva that can be eaten as 'bush tucker'

14. Which major line of latitude runs through Australia?
    A) Equator B) Tropic of Cancer C) Tropic of Capricorn

15. Which British rock star played Ned Kelly in the 1970 film about the infamous Australian bandit?
    A) David Bowie B) Mick Jagger C) Ringo Starr

16. What is unusual about wombat poo?
    A) It's bright purple
    B) It's cube shaped
    C) There's a lot of it, as wombats always defecate in the same place

17. Which of these is not an Australian wine region?
    A) Hunter Valley B) Yarra Valley C) Marlborough

18. Every year, the Australian territory of Christmas Island sees a mass migration of which animal?
    A) Kangaroos B) Crabs C) Jellyfish

19. Which Australian author won the Booker Prize for literature in 1982 for *Schindler's Ark*?

20. The town of Coober Pedy lies at the centre of the world's main mining area for what colourful gemstone?
    A) Opal B) Lapis Lazuli C) Tourmaline

Quiz 36 **General Travel Knowledge**

1. *Journey to the West*, also known as *Monkey* in one of its most famous translations, is a classic 16th-century novel from which country?
   A) Japan B) China C) India

2. In London, on the banks of the Thames, stands one of a pair of ancient obelisks that were removed from Egypt in the 19th century. Both are known Cleopatra's Needle. Where is the other one situated?
   A) Paris, France B) New York, USA C) Auckland, New Zealand

3. For most of his career, the Brazilian footballer Pelé played for which South American club team?
   A) São Paulo FC B) Santos C) Boca Juniors

4. At the end of his career, Pelé played two seasons for which US soccer team?
   A) New York Cosmos
   B) Los Angeles Aztecs
   C) Tampa Bay Rowdies

5. Gibraltar, the tiny British territory on the southern coast of Spain, is home to a colony of what non-indigenous species of monkey?
   A) Colobus monkeys B) Emperor tamarins C) Barbary apes

6. The citizens of the Caribbean territories of Aruba, Sint Maarten and Curaçao are all nationals of which country?

7. What nationality were the writers George Bernard Shaw and Oscar Wilde?

8. The markhor is the national animal of Pakistan. What sort of animal is it?
   A) A bird of prey B) A goat C) A snake

9. According to a 17th-century law, what colour must all the gondolas in Venice be painted?

10. In Budapest, Hungary, there's a life-size bronze statue of which 1970s US TV detective?
    A) Columbo B) Kojak C) Hutch (from *Starsky and Hutch*)

11. The airport of which city sells the most chocolate in the world?
    A) Zurich, Switzerland B) Brussels, Belgium C) Barcelona, Spain

12. By area, what is the largest US state?

13. Considered a living god by followers of the Rastafari movement in Jamaica, how was Ras Tafari Makonnen better known?

14. The French emperor Napoleon Bonaparte was exiled twice in his life to two different islands, the second time permanently. Can you name both islands? You get a point for each.

15. In 1980, the territory of New Hebrides in the South Pacific changed its name to what upon gaining independence?

16. Prior to 1980, New Hebrides had been a colony of which country?
    A) The UK B) France C) Both the UK and France

17. In 1984, the Republic of Upper Volta in Africa changed its name to what?

18. What does orangutan mean in the Malay language?
    A) Man of the forest B) Orange ape C) Long-haired friend

19. By what name is the humanitarian organisation the Red Cross known in Islamic countries?

20. With an estimated population of 1.5 billion individuals, the red-billed quelea is believed to be the world's most common wild bird. In what continent would you find it?
    A) South America B) Africa C) Asia

Quiz 37 **Boats and Ships**

1. From which city did the *Titanic* depart on her maiden voyage
    on 10 April, 1912?
    A) Belfast, Northern Ireland
    B) Southampton, England
    C) Cherbourg, France

2. The Polynesian islands were settled from around 1000 BCE onwards by
    people using double-hull and outrigger canoes. What is an outrigger?
    A) A large sail that can catch more wind than a normal sail
    B) An extra float on the side of the hull, providing stability
    C) A type of tree that produces extremely buoyant wood

3. Now a popular visitor attraction in Greenwich, London, the
    Cutty Sark was a super-fast 19th-century sailing ship, or clipper,
    designed to transport what commodity?
    A) Tea B) Wool C) Coal

4. In 1955, British engineer Christopher Cockerell invented what
    water-transport vehicle?
    A) Roll-on roll-off ferry B) Trimaran C) Hovercraft

5. What was the name of the ship on Captain Cook's first voyage of
    discovery to Australia and New Zealand in 1768–71?
    A) HMS *Endeavour* B) HMS *Discovery* C) HMS *Terra Nova*

6. Which writer first used the term 'Ship of Fools' to describe an
    incompetent government?
    A) Plato B) Machiavelli C) Shakespeare

7. What was the name of the Norwegian explorer who in the 1940s
    undertook a 6900km (4300 mile) journey from South America
    to Polynesia on the wooden raft, *Kon-Tiki*?

8. The *Mary Rose,* a Tudor warship of King Henry VIII, sank off
    the south coast of England in 1545. In what decade of the
    20th century was it brought back to the surface?
    A) 1940s B) 1960s C) 1980s

9. In which English city is the *Mary Rose* now on display?
   A) Plymouth B) Portsmouth C) Chatham

10. What is the name of the whaling ship of Captain Ahab in Herman Melville's epic novel *Moby Dick*?

11. According to the Bible, how many cubits long was Noah's Ark?
    A) 200 B) 300 C) 400

12. In the nonsense poem by Edward Lear, the Owl and the Pussy-Cat went to sea in what colour boat?

13. In Oslo, Norway, you can visit a museum dedicated to what?
    A) Container ships B) Viking ships C) Naval ships

14. In the sea shanty popularised by Robert Louis Stevenson in *Treasure Island*, how many men were on a dead man's chest?
    A) Fifteen B) Fifty C) Sixty

15. Where did the submersible DSV *Limiting Factor* visit in 2019?
    A) The bottom of Mariana Trench
    B) The ocean below the Antarctic ice shelf
    C) The scalding waters of black smokers on the Mid-Atlantic Ridge

16. What was the name of the ship built by King Caspian X of Narnia in the books by C.S. Lewis?

17. What was the ship that took Charles Darwin on the voyages that led to him formulating his theory of evolution by natural selection?

18. The *Orca* is a ship featured in which Hollywood film?
    A) *Life of Pi* B) *The Big Blue* C) *Jaws*

19. Discovered in 2022 after it sank in 1917, *Endurance* is the ship used by which British explorer on his journey to Antarctica?
    A) Robert Falcon Scott B) Ernest Shackleton C) Henry Hudson

20. In the British TV series, what was Captain Pugwash's ship?
    A) *Black Pig* B) *Coddling Catfish* C) *Cut-Throat Jake*

Quiz 38 **The Caribbean**

1. What is the capital of Barbados?
    A) Kingston B) Bridgetown C) St John's

2. The reggae singer Bob Marley hailed from which Caribbean island?

3. Cuba is supposedly the birthplace of the mojito, a cocktail made from rum, lime, sugar and what else?
    A) Crushed cherries B) Olives C) Mint

4. What is special about Juancho E. Yrausquin Airport (SAB) on the island of Saba, a Netherlands overseas region?
    A) It sits on the ocean on a floating platform
    B) It has the world's shortest commercial runway
    C) No planes have ever landed here, as it was built and then immediately abandoned

5. Which island in the Caribbean region has a name that means 'Rich Port'?

6. On average, how many hurricanes occur in the Caribbean each year?
    A) Six B) Sixteen C) Sixty

7. Found on numerous Caribbean islands, what is the name of this bird, known for its bright red throat pouch, which the males inflate to attract females?
    A) Magnificent frigatebird B) Brown pelican C) Wandering albatross

8. Port-au-Prince is the capital of which Caribbean country?

9. What is the style of cooking developed in Jamaica in which meat is prepared with a mixture of allspice and scotch bonnet peppers?
A) Jerk B) Pattie C) Ackee

10. To what country does the Caribbean island of Montserrat belong?
A) France B) UK C) Spain

11. How many inhabited US territories are there in the Caribbean?
A) One B) Two C) Three

12. Which Caribbean country removed the British Queen, Elizabeth II, as head of state in 2021 to become a republic?

13. A native of Guadeloupe is a citizen of which country?
A) The UK B) France C) The Netherlands

14. What is the most southerly Caribbean island country?
A) St Lucia B) Grenada C) Trinidad and Tobago

15. What is Barbados' national dish?
A) Green banana and saltfish
B) Flying fish and coucou
C) Fungee and pepperpot

16. How many islands make up St Vincent and the Grenadines?
A) 12 B) 22 C) 32

17. Which Caribbean country was invaded by the US in 1983?

18. By both area and population, what is the largest country in the Caribbean?

19. By population, what is the smallest independent country in the Caribbean
A) Saint Kitts and Nevis B) Dominica C) Antigua and Barbuda

20. Desnoes & Geddes is the manufacturer of what famous Caribbean drink?
A) Bacardi rum B) Red Stripe beer C) Tia Maria coffee liqueur

Quiz 39 **Film Locations Around the World**

1. The climax of the 1959 Alfred Hitchcock film *North by Northwest* takes place on top of which US landmark?
    A) Statue of Liberty B) Empire State Building C) Mount Rushmore

2. In what country were the three Lord of the Rings movies that were released between 2001–03 filmed?

3. What 1972 thriller centred on three friends canoeing down a river in Georgia, USA?
    A) *The Poseidon Adventure* B) *Deliverance* C) *Jeremiah Johnson*

4. The harbour wall, or Cobb, in the English seaside town of Lyme Regis is the setting for an iconic scene in which 1981 film of a John Fowles novel?

5. The 1999 horror film *The Blair Witch Project* is about three friends hiking in the Black Hills of which US state?
    A) Maryland B) Virginia C) Georgia

6. *Parasite*, the film that won the 2020 Best Picture Oscar, is set in which Asian city?
    A) Tokyo, Japan B) Beijing, China C) Seoul, South Korea

7. In what country was the classic Hollywood film *Casablanca*, starring Humphrey Bogart and Ingrid Bergman, filmed?
    A) Morocco B) France C) USA

8. The 2002 film *City of God* is set in which South American city?
    A) Lima, Peru B) Bogotá, Colombia C) Rio de Janeiro, Brazil

9. In the 1969 crime caper *The Italian Job*, Michael Caine leads a criminal gang in a daring robbery in which Italian city?
    A) Rome B) Turin C) Milan

10. Scenes from the first six Star Wars movies were filmed in which North African country?

11. The 1993 film, *The Piano,* which won several Oscars, is largely set in which Pacific country?
A) New Zealand B) Australia C) Tonga

12. Which English seaside resort features heavily in the 1979 film *Quadrophenia*, based on a rock opera by The Who?

13. The 1982 German film *Fitzcarraldo* centres on an attempt to transport a steamship over a hill to a rubber plantation in which South American country?
A) Brazil B) Argentina C) Peru

14. The iconic car chase scene in the 1968 film *Bullitt* was filmed in which US city?
A) San Francisco B) Los Angeles C) Chicago

15. The 2009 Best Picture Oscar winner, *Slumdog Millionaire* tells the rags to riches story of a TV quiz show contestant from which Indian city?
A) Delhi B) Mumbai C) Kolkata

16. Which American landmark famously features in the final scene of the original 1968 *Planet of the Apes*?

17. The 2009 Iranian drama *About Elly*, is largely set next to which large body of water?
A) Black Sea B) Mediterranean Sea C) Caspian Sea

18. In which city was the 2003 film *Lost in Translation* set?
A) New York, USA B) Paris, France C) Tokyo, Japan

19. Despite its title, the 2014 film *The Grand Budapest Hotel* isn't actually set in Hungary but in the fictional country of what?
A) Amity Island B) Zubrowka C) Mos Eisley

20. In 2008, Colin Farrell starred in a thriller set in, and named after, which European city?

Quiz 40 **Seas and Oceans**

1. What is the world's largest ocean?

1. And what is the world's smallest ocean?

3. Challenger Deep is the deepest known point on the seabed. It's found in the Pacific Ocean at the bottom of what trench?

4. Just how deep is the deepest point of the ocean?
   A) 5,935m (19,472ft)
   B) 10,935m (35,876ft)
   C) 15,935m (52,280ft)

5. What sea occupies the lowest point on land, 430.5m (1412ft) below sea level?
   A) The Dead Sea B) The Black Sea C) The Red Sea

6. What is the world's largest inland sea?
   A) The Caspian Sea B) The Aral Sea C) The Sea of Azov

7. What is the world's saltiest sea?
   A) The Sargasso Sea B) The Dead Sea C) The Bering Sea

8. Which sea divides Africa from the Arabian Peninsula?

9. Which canal connects the Atlantic and the Pacific Ocean?

10. Where would you find the Sea of Tranquillity?

11. Which three oceans border the USA?

12. In 1927, who became the first person to fly solo across the Atlantic Ocean?
    A) Louis Blériot B) Amy Johnson C) Charles Lindbergh

13. The Laccadive Sea, the Andaman Sea and the Gulf of Aden are all part of which ocean?

14. The Tasman Sea separates the mainland of Australia from the island of Tasmania. True or false?

15. What is the only ocean that blue whales do not inhabit?

16. 'I must go down to the seas again, to the lonely sea and the sky' are the first words of a famous poem by which poet?
A) WH Auden B) John Masefield C) Percy Bysshe Shelley

17. What was the name of the easternmost sea in the Narnia books by C.S Lewis?
A) The Gold Sea B) The Silver Sea C) The Bronze Sea

18. The name 'Mediterranean' derives from Latin words meaning what?
A) Middle of the Earth B) Deep Blue Water C) Wet and Wavy

19. What is unusual about the Sargasso Sea?
A) It doesn't have any borders
B) It's permanently covered in a layer of glowing algae
C) It's completely lifeless

20. Narwhals, such as the one shown here, mainly inhabit which ocean?

Quiz 41 **True or False?**

All you have to do in this quiz is work out whether the
statements below are true or a great big fib.

1. Scotland's national animal is the Loch Ness Monster.

2. We're closer in time to Queen Cleopatra of Egypt than she was
    to the building of the Great Pyramid at Giza.

3. The Great Wall of China is so large that it can be seen from space
    with the naked eye.

4. The continental USA is wider than the Moon.

5. The Channel Tunnel between England and France is the world's
    longest rail tunnel.

6. When the first hot-air balloon took to the skies in France, 1783,
    its first passengers were a sheep, a duck and a rooster.

7. It takes 15 days to ride the world's longest rail route, the Trans-
    Siberian Railway, across the full width of Russia.

8. Over half of the Earth's landmass is desert.

9. The deepest hole ever dug went a fifth of the way to the centre
    of the Earth.

10. Every year, more people visit Thailand than any other country.

11. Japan has suffered more earthquakes than any other country.

12. Just 3% of Earth's total amount of water is salt water.

13. Spain's Canary Islands were named after dogs, not birds.

14. The USA is the only country in the world that doesn't use the
    metric system.

15. The town of Mawsynram in India, is the world's driest inhabited place, having last seen rain in 1902.

16. This is an image of Venice, Italy

17. Jamaica has the only national flag that does not contain the colours red, white or blue.

18. Sweden has more islands than any other country.

19. More people have walked on the Moon (12) than have been to the bottom of Earth's ocean (3).

20. A quarter of all the people that have ever lived are alive right now.

21. The people of New Zealand have more pets per household than any other country.

22. In Russia, beer is not classed as an alcoholic beverage.

23. The Moon is gradually getting closer to Earth. This is increasing its gravitational pull and speeding up the planet's rotation. This means the days are gradually getting shorter by just under two milliseconds every century.

24. A cross between a jaguar and a leopard is known as a jaglep.

25. A hurricane, a typhoon and a tropical cyclone are all exactly the same thing.

Quiz 42 **West Africa**

1. According to the United Nations, West Africa is made up of how many countries?
   A) 8 B) 16 C) 24

2. What is the most widely spoken language in West Africa?
   A) French B) English C) Arabic

3. Not as widely spoken, what is the official language of the island country of Cape Verde?
   A) Spanish B) Portuguese C) Italian

4. What is the only West African country that has Arabic as its official language?
   A) Benin B) Guinea-Bissau C) Mauritania

5. Around how many languages are spoken in Nigeria? And, for a bonus point, what is the official language?
   A) 50 B) 500 C) 5000

6. Discovered in the 1970s in the deserts of Niger, Nigersaurus is what sort of dinosaur?
   A) A sauropod, like diplodocus
   B) A theropod, like Tyrannosaurus Rex
   C) An ornithischian, like Triceratops

7. In what country would you find the medieval city of Timbuktu?
   A) Mali B) The Gambia C) Togo

8. In what year did Ghana achieve independence from the UK?
   A) 1957 B) 1967 C) 1977

9. The traditional West African stringed instrument known as a kora has how many strings?
   A) 2 B) 22 C) 222

10. What is the capital of Sierra Leone?
    A) Newtown B) Sierra Town C) Freetown

11. The flag and constitution of which country are largely based on those of the USA?
    A) Côte d'Ivoire B) Liberia C) Sierra Leone

12. King Mansa Mūsā who ruled Mali in the 14th century has what legendary claim to fame?
    A) He may have been the tallest person who ever lived
    B) He supposedly swam around the entire coast of Africa
    C) He may have been the richest person who ever lived

13. The Senegalese singer Youssou N'Dour achieved a worldwide hit in 1993 with which song, a duet with Neneh Cherry?
    A) '4 5 Seconds' B) '7 Seconds' C) '24 Hours from Tulsa'

14. Yamoussoukro is the capital of which West African country?

15. Known as the 'Giant of Africa', which West African country is the most populous nation on the whole continent?

16. What international position did the Ghanaian Kofi Annan hold from 1997 to 2006?
    A) Secretary General of the United Nations
    B) President of the International Olympic Committee
    C) CEO of Coca Cola

17. What is West Africa's longest river, the third longest in Africa?

18. Described by Lonely Planet as West Africa's 'best wildlife park', in what country would you find the Parc National de la Pendjari?
    A) Benin B) Mali C) The Gambia

19. In which country would you find people wearing a traditional woven cloth known as Kente?
    A) Burkina Faso B) Ghana C) Togo

20. In 2006, Ellen Johnson Sirleaf became the first female elected head of state in Africa when she became president of which country?
    A) Liberia B) Mauritania C) Nigeria

Quiz 43 **Castles, Palaces and Fortresses**

1. Built in the mid-19th century from the ruins of a monastery, the colourful Pena Palace sits on top of a hill in which Portuguese town?
    A) Sintra B) Olhão C) Silves

2. Which country has the most number of castles per square kilometre in the world?
    A) Wales B) Germany C) France

3. The official residence of Russia's monarchs between 1732 and 1917, the Winter Palace is located in which city?
    A) Moscow B) Saint Petersburg C) Vladivostok

4. Ustad Ahmad Lahori, the architect of the Taj Mahal, is also usually credited as the designer of which famous Mughal fortress?
    A) Lake Palace, Udaipur B) Mysore Palace C) The Red Fort, Delhi

5. Which Scandinavian castle was the inspiration for Hamlet's home in Shakespeare's play?
    A) The Royal Palace, Stockholm, Sweden
    B) Akershus Fortress, Oslo, Norway
    C) Kronborg Castle, Helsingør, Denmark

6. The castle of Fasil Ghebbi was which African country's royal residence from the 1640s to the 1840s?
    A) Egypt B) Ethiopia C) Namibia

7. Which French king was responsible for transforming Versailles from a small chateau to a grand palace between 1661 and 1715?
    A) Louis X B) Louis XIV C) Louis XVIII

8. The medieval fortress city of Great Zimbabwe gives the modern African country its name. What does 'Zimbabwe' translate as?
    A) Tall towers B) Stone houses C) Royal palace

9. Identify the Asian palace from the description: A vast wooden complex of almost 1,000 buildings, its famous landmarks include the Meridian Gate and the Hall of Supreme Harmony.

10. In what Italian city would you find the Doge's Palace?

11. Himeji Castle is considered one of the most beautiful and
    well-preserved castles in Japan. What colour are its walls?
    A) White B) Red C) Black

12. By land area, Malbork Castle is the largest castle in the world.
    In which country would you find it?
    A) England B) Germany C) Poland

13. Which UK royal castle is the largest occupied castle in the world?
    A) Warwick Castle B) Windsor Castle C) Edinburgh Castle

14. The Citadel of Aleppo in Syria is believed to be one of the oldest
    castles in the world. In what millennium did construction begin?
    A) First B) Third C) Fifth

15. The Topkapı Palace in Istanbul, Turkey, was the royal residence of
    the rulers of which empire between 1478 and 1856?
    A) Ottoman B) Byzantine C) Roman

16. The only royal palace in the USA is found in which state?
    A) California B) Hawaii C) Florida

17. The Grand Palace in Bangkok, Thailand, is home to the Temple
    of the Emerald what?
    A) Snake C) Elephant C) Buddha

18. The American president has the White House, but what colour is
    palatial mansion where the Argentinian president has their office?
    A) Pink B) Purple C) Yellow

19. What real-life Romanian castle is said to have provided author
    Bram Stoker with the inspiration for his fictional 'Castle Dracula'?
    A) Transylvania Castle B) Castle Draco C) Bran Castle

20. The 18th-century Hawa Mahal in Jaipur, India, which boasts over
    900 windows, is also known as what?
    A) Palace of the Windows B) Palace of the Winds C) Pink Palace

Quiz 44 **Sydney**

1. In what year was Sydney founded?
   A) 1688 B) 1788 C) 1888

2. Sydney is located in which state?
   A) Victoria B) New South Wales C) South Australia

3. What is the clothing-themed nickname of the iconic Sydney Harbour Bridge?
   A) The Hat Stand B) The Shoe Tree C) The Coathanger

4. It was based on which British bridge that had opened just a few years earlier?
   A) Tyne Bridge, Newcastle
   B) Tower Bridge, London
   C) Forth Bridge, Edinburgh

5. By what name are the residents of Sydney popularly known?
   A) Sydneysupporters B) Sydneysiders C) Sydneyites

6. In what year did Sydney Opera House open?
   A) 1953 B) 1973 C) 1993

7. What was the nationality of its architect?
   A) Australian B) Chinese C) Danish

8. What is the name of the Australian Football League team that play their home games at the Sydney Cricket Ground?
   A) Sydney Swans B) GWS Giants C) Sydney Saints

9. Which actor, a star of the X-Men film series, was born in Sydney?

10. Australia's oldest daily newspaper is published in Sydney. What is its name?
    A) *Sydney Morning Herald* B) *Sydney Times* C) *Sydney Telegraph*

11. What percentage of Australia's population lives in Sydney?
    A) 5% B) 20% C) 50%

12. Which is Sydney's largest beach?
    A) Bondi Beach B) Manly Beach C) Bate Bay

13. Established in 1850, The University of Sydney is the country's oldest university. True or false?

14. In what year did Sydney host the Summer Olympic Games?
    A) 1920 B) 1960 C) 2000

15. What is Sydney's tallest structure?
    A) Crown Sydney B) Chifley Tower C) Sydney Tower

16. Sydney is home to Australia's oldest museum, founded back in 1827. What is its name?
    A) The Museum of Sydney
    B) The Australian Museum
    C) The Powerhouse Museum

17. It's nearly 3300km (2050 miles) from Perth on the west coast of Australia to Sydney on the east. How many hours ahead of Perth is Sydney?
    A) Two B) Four C) Six

18. On average, how many days of rain does sunny Sydney endure each year?
    A) 20 B) 70 C) 100

19. Before going on to achieve worldwide fame, which rock group made its debut in Sydney on New Year's Eve, 1973?
    A) Midnight Oil B) INXS C) AC/DC

20. What medical device was invented in 1926 by Sydney resident, Dr Mark Lidwill?
    A) The pacemaker B) The replacement hip C) The stethoscope

Quiz 45 **Deserts**

1. To be classed as a desert, an area has to receive less than how much precipitation a year
   A) 2.5cm (1 inch) B) 25cm (10 inches) C) 50cm (20 inches)

2. What is the world's largest desert?
   A) Sahara Desert B) Antarctica C) Gobi Desert

3. What is the world's driest desert?
   A) Atacama Desert B) Namib Desert C) Simpson Desert

4. The Gobi Desert covers parts of which two Asian countries?

5. The Namib Desert covers parts of Namibia, South Africa and which other African nation?
   A) Angola B) Zimbabwe C) Zambia

6. The Thar Desert covers parts of Pakistan and what other Asian country?

7. Most of the Chihuahuan Desert lies in which country?
   A) Mexico B) Guatemala C) USA

8. The Kalahari Desert covers parts of three African nations. Which of these is not one of them?
   A) South Africa B) Botswana C) Mozambique

9. The name 'Kalahari' is a word from the language of the Tswana people of Southern Africa. What does it mean?
   A) Super Dry B) Great Thirst C) Sandy Hills

10. In what country would you find the Taklamakan Desert?
    A) Peru B) Morocco C) China

11. What is the only continent that doesn't have a major desert?

12. What is the largest desert in the USA?
    A) Mojave Desert B) Great Basin Desert C) Sonoran Desert

13. Meerkats are desert animals from which continent?

14. Which desert contains the longest expanse of unbroken sand?
    A) Arabian Desert B) Pinnacles Desert C) Syrian Desert

15. Which ocean-front desert is famous for its Skeleton Coast, which has been the site of numerous shipwrecks?

16. What percentage of Australia is desert?
    A) 8% B) 18% C) 28%

17. What is the largest Australian desert?
    A) Tanami Desert B) Great Sandy Desert C) Great Victoria Desert

18. Saguaro cacti, such as the ones shown below, can only be found living the wild in the deserts of which continent?

19. Which of these is not a hot desert?
    A) Gobi Desert B) Sahara Desert C) Thar Desert

20. In what country would you find the Lut Desert where land surface temperatures of 70.7°C (159.3°F) have been recorded, the hottest of the 21st century
    A) Saudi Arabia B) Iran C) Pakistan

Quiz 46 **France**

1. On what date does France celebrate its national day, commonly known abroad as Bastille Day?
   A) 4 July B) 14 July C) 25 December

2. What is the longest river to flow wholly through France?
   A) The Seine B) The Rhine C) The Loire

3. What does the name of France's best-selling newspaper, *Le Monde*, mean?
   A) The World B) The Mountain C) The Opinion

4. What was France's currency before it adopted the euro in 2002?

5. What are the colours of the French flag?
   A) Red, white and green
   B) Red, white and blue
   C) Red, yellow and black

6. The motto of France is *Liberté* (Liberty) *Égalité* (Equality) and what else?
   A) *Humanité* (Humanity) B) *Vérité* (Truth) C) *Fraternité* (Fraternity)

7. What colour jersey does the rider who has been named 'King of the Mountains' in the Tour de France wear?
   A) Yellow B) Green C) Red polka dots

8. The tradition of playing pranks on 1 April, known in English as 'April Fools' is known in French as what?
   A) *Poisson d'Avril* B) *Vache d'Avril* C) *Chien d'Avril*

9. Marie Antoinette, the last Queen of France before the French Revolution, was married to which King?
   A) Louis XIV B) Louis XVI C) Charles X

10. Both the king and queen were executed in the French Revolution that began in what year of the 18th century?

11. The painting commemorating the later 1830 Revolution known as
    Liberty Leading the People is by which artist?
    A) Renoir B) Delacroix C) David

12. Which of Victor Hugo's novels, later a smash-hit musical, is set
    during the failed 1832 rebellion?

13. By population, what is France's second-largest city?
    A) Lyon B) Marseille C) Paris

14. Veuve Cliquot is a brand of which type of French wine?
    A) Red B) White C) Champagne

15. What is France's highest mountain?

16. This gargoyle sits atop what medieval Parisian cathedral, which
    suffered a devastating fire in 2019?

17. France shares Lake Geneva with what other country? And, for a
    bonus point, what is the French name for the lake?

18. Which French singer had the nickname, 'The Little Sparrow'?

19. Which French theme park is based on the works of Uderzo
    and Goscinny?
    A) Disneyland Paris B) Parc Astérix C) Futuroscope

20. Known as *Call my Agent!* internationally, by what name is the
    hit TV show known in France?
    A) *Dix Pour Cent* B) *Le Bureau* C) *On va s'aimer un peu, beaucoup*

Quiz 47 **The Wide World of Sports**

1. Which city hosted the first modern Olympic Games in 1896?

2. The Ryōgoku Kokugikan arena in Tokyo is the main venue for which Japanese sport?
    A) Aikido B) Karate C) Sumo

3. The Tour de France cycling event is staged over how many days?
    A) 7 B) 14 C) 23

4. The Ashes is an international cricket competition between which two nations?

5. One of the greatest football players of all time, the Argentinian Diego Maradona represented three European clubs over the course of his career. Can you name them?

6. The quarterback Tom Brady has won the Superbowl seven times, with which two teams?

7. Can you name the only three Swiss players to have won tennis grand slam tournaments? You get a point for each.

8. What two nations hosted the FIFA Men's World Cup in 2002?

9. Of the four 'major' golf tournaments played each year, only one is always held at the same venue. In what US city is it located?

10. The gold, silver and bronze medal winners at the 2020 Olympic Women's 100 metre final all represented which country?
    A) USA B) Jamaica C) France

11. Which countries compete in the international rugby union tournament known as the Six Nations? You get a point for each.

12. The Lions, the Pistons and the Tigers represent which US city in, respectively, the sports of American football, basketball and baseball?

13. The World Chess Championship of 1972 between the Soviet Boris Spassky and the American Bobby Fischer, known as the 'Match of the Century', was held in which city?
    A) Zurich, Switzerland B) Reykjavík, Iceland C) Tokyo, Japan

14. The 'Fight of the Century' between Muhammad Ali and Joe Frazier for the Heavyweight Championship of the World in 1971 was staged at what famous New York venue?
    A) Radio City B) Yankee Stadium C) Madison Square Garden

15. What is the oldest international sporting trophy?
    A) The Ryder Cup B) The FIFA World Cup C) The America's Cup

16. What is the name and location of this famous sporting stadium?
    A) Wembley Stadium, London, England
    B) Camp Nou, Barcelona, Spain
    C) The Waca, Perth, Australia

17. The four most prestigious annual tennis tournaments, also known as the 'Grand Slam' events are held in which countries? You get a point for each.

18. What city hosted the Olympic Games in 1908, 1948 and 2012?

19. The Calcutta Cup is a trophy awarded to the annual winner of a match between England and Scotland in which sport?
    A) Snooker B) Rugby Union C) Darts

20. Oleksandr Usyk and Vasiliy Lomachenko are both world champions boxers from which country?

Quiz 48 **Explorers and Voyages of Discovery**

1. Who is believed to have been the first European to set foot on the continent of North America?
   A) Leif Erikson B) Christopher Columbus C) John Cabot

2. Who was the first person to see the continent of Antarctica?
   A) Roald Amundsen
   B) Fabian Gottlieb von Bellingshausen
   C) Robert Falcon Scott

3. What was the name of the mission that put the first people on the Moon in 1969?
   A) Apollo 5 B) Apollo 11 C) Apollo 17

4. In 1889–90, the American journalist Nellie Bly undertook a round-the world trip inspired by which recently published novel?

5. In what year did Julius Caesar become the first Roman leader to set foot in Britain?
   A) 55 BCE B) 43 CE C) 410 CE

6. What was the name of the ship in which Sir Francis Drake circumnavigated the globe from 1577–1580
   A) *Victoria* B) *Golden Hind* C) *Santa Maria*

7. In what modern-day country did the explorer Henry Morton Stanley find the then missing explorer, David Livingstone?
   A) Kenya B) Uganda C) Tanzania

8. In what century did the Chinese explorer Zheng He undertake a decades long 'treasure voyage' across Asia and East Africa?
   A) 10th B) 15th C) 19th

9. On what archipelago was the British explorer Captain James Cook killed in 1779?
   A) Hawaii B) Galápagos Islands C) Kiribati

10. What nationality was round-the-world explorer Ferdinand Magellan?

11. In 2021, Emily Ford became the first woman and the first person of colour to trek the Ice Age Trail in winter. A route of nearly 2000km (1200 miles) along the glacial line of the last ice age, in what US state does the trail lie?
A) Alaska B) Washington C) Wisconsin

12. George Everest, the man after whom the world's tallest peak is named, never visited – or even saw – the mountain. True or false?

13. The first people to climb Mount Everest were Edmund Hillary and who else, a Sherpa from Nepal?

14. The Lewis and Clark Expedition across the USA from 1803–06 was inspired by what land deal, in which the American government bought a huge swathe of North American territory from France?

15. In 1932, the American aviator Amelia Earhart became the first woman to fly solo across what body of water?
A) English Channel B) Atlantic Ocean C) The Pacific Ocean

16. In 1594, the British explorer Sir Walter Raleigh sailed to South America to try and find which mythical 'City of Gold'?
A) Elysium B) El Dorado C) Atlantis

17. The American Matthew Henson may have been the first person to set foot where?
A) The North Pole B) The source of the Nile C) Machu Picchu

18. Which of these Polynesian countries was settled last?
A) New Zealand B) Hawaii C) Tonga

19. What was the name of the captain who was cast adrift in a small boat after a mutiny aboard his ship *Bounty* during a voyage to Tahiti in the 18th century?

20. What is the English translation of the book in which the 13th-century Italian explorer Marco Polo described his travels in Asia?
A) *Across Asia on the Cheap* B) *The Million* C) *Book of Marvels*

Quiz 49 **Southeast Asia**

1. According to the UN, how many countries make up Southeast Asia?
    A) Nine B) Ten C) Eleven

2. By area, what is the largest country in Southeast Asia?
    A) Myanmar (Burma) B) Malaysia C) Indonesia

3. By population, what is the largest country in Southeast Asia?
    A) Thailand B) Vietnam C) Indonesia

4. By area, what is the smallest country in Southeast Asia?
    A) Brunei B) Singapore C) East Timor

5. By population, what is the smallest country in Southeast Asia
    A) Brunei B) Singapore C) East Timor

6. By population, what is the largest city in Southeast Asia?
    A) Manila, Philippines B) Bangkok, Thailand C) Jakarta, Indonesia

7. What three nations share the island of Borneo?

8. What is the currency of Thailand?
    A) The Baht B) The Riel C) The Rupiah

9. What is the capital of Cambodia?

10. In what country would you find this precariously balanced temple?

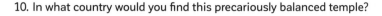

11. Vietnam is the world's largest exporter of which nut?
    A) Peanut B) Pistachio C) Cashew

12. The Philippines is the world's largest exporter of which oil?
    A) Palm oil B) Coconut oil C) Sunflower oil

13. What is the name of the Indonesian volcano which exploded in 1883, producing what is believed to be the loudest noise in recorded history?

14. In what country would you find Hang Son Đoòng, the world's largest cave?
    A) Vietnam B) Laos C) Kiribati

15. In what city would you find the twin skyscraper, the Petronas Towers, once the tallest building in the world?

16. What is the longest river in Southeast Asia?
    A) Mekong B) Irrawaddy C) Red River

17. What is Vietnam's national dish, a soup made with meat, broth and rice noodles?
    A) Cha ca B) Banh xeo C) Pho

18. Found in the Philippines, Malaysia, Indonesia and Brunei, what sort of animal is a tarsier?
    A) A primate B) A crab C) A bat

19. Can you name the five countries with which Laos shares a land border?

20. Indonesia is made up of approximately how many islands?
    A) 170 B) 1700 C) 17,000

Quiz 50 **Silhouette Cities**

Can identify which city these silhouette compilations of major landmarks represent from the three available options?

1.

A) Cairo, Egypt
B) Cape Town, South Africa
C) Nairobi, Kenya

2.

A) Berlin, Germany
B) Paris, France
C) London, England

3.

A) Tokyo, Japan
B) Stockholm , Sweden
C) Auckland, New Zealand

4.

A) Toronto, Canada
B) Washington DC, USA
C) Mexico City, Mexico

5.

A) Rio de Janeiro, Brazil
B) St Petersburg, Russia
C) Athens, Greece

6.

A) Delhi, India
B) St Petersburg, Russia
C) Kingston, Jamaica

- Cities -

7.

A) Venice, Italy
B) Oxford, England
C) Las Vegas, USA

8.

A) Miami, USA
B) Vancouver, Canada
C) Lima, Peru

9.

A) Moscow, Russia
B) Prague, Czech Republic
C) Edinburgh, Scotland

10.

A) Bogotá, Colombia
B) Amsterdam, The Netherlands
C) Sydney, Australia

11.

A) Singapore
B) Shanghai, China
C) Dubai, UAE

12.

A) Madrid, Spain
B) Rome, Italy
C) Oslo, Norway

13.

B) Brussels, Belgium
C) Marrakesh, Morocco
A) Buenos Aires, Argentina

14.

A) Istanbul , Turkey
B) Beijing, China
C) Moscow, Russia

15.

A) Budapest, Hungary
B) Hong Kong, China
C) Caracas, Venezuela

Quiz 51 **Guess the Country**

Can you work out what each country is from the clues?

1. This country includes the westernmost point in mainland Europe. Its famous exports include cork, fortified wine and *Pastéis de Nata*.

2. A country in the Middle East named after a famous river, it has many ancient archaeological and religious sites, including Petra and Mount Nebo.

3. Nicknamed 'the hexagon', this country is the largest by area in the EU. It is home to the most visited museum in the world and has won the most Nobel Prizes for Literature.

4. This Caribbean island is a popular holiday destination. The nation's biggest cultural event of the year is called Crop Over, a festival celebrating the island's calypso music and cuisine.

5. Although a small country, this European nation boasts eight national parks and 12 nature parks. Its popular city destinations include Zagreb and Split.

6. The fourth largest island in the world, this African nation is home to many unique species, including lemurs and chameleons.

7. This densely forested Nordic country is reputedly the world's happiest nation. It's also known as the 'land of a thousand lakes'.

8. This vast, landlocked country is located between Russia and China. A giant statue depicting the country's founder on horseback sits outside the capital city.

9. An island nation off the east coast of Asia, made up of four main islands and numerous smaller ones, it is home to many castles and mountains, not to mention the highest density of vending machines in the world.

10. This West African nation is the most populated country in Africa. Its film industry, Nollywood, is one of the largest in the world.

11. Around 80% of the world's cinnamon is produced in this South Asian island country, formerly known as Ceylon.

12. A Central Asian country whose capital is Tashkent, it is one of only two nations in the world that is doubly landlocked.

13. Almost half of this nation is covered in the Amazon rainforest. Famous destinations in the country include the Inca ruins of Machu Picchu and the Nazca lines.

14. This country has the world's largest population of Spanish speakers. An annual holiday, *Día de los Muertos*, is usually celebrated on the 1st and 2nd of November.

15. The second largest country in the world, this huge nation spans six time zones. More than half of all the lakes in the world can be found here.

16. An East African country famous for its wildlife parks and reserves – it has over 50. These include Masai Mara National Park and the Nairobi National Park.

17. This Central American country is known for its incredible biodiversity and numerous national parks. Its capital is San José.

18. The highest mountain range in the world, the Himalayas, rises in the north of this country. It is the only country in the world with native populations of both lions and tigers.

19. This remote nation consists of two main islands – North Island and South Island. It was the first country in the world to give women the right to vote.

20. One of the largest nations in South America, the name of this country's capital city translates as 'good airs' or 'fair winds'.

Quiz 52 **Central and Southern Africa**

1. What geographical feature covers most of South Africa?
   A) A desert B) A plateau C) A valley

2. From which country did the Central African Republic gain independence in 1960?
   A) France B) Portugal C) UK

3. Native to the Ituri Rainforest in the Democratic Republic of Congo, by what name is the 'forest giraffe' more commonly known?
   A) Okapi B) Tapir C) Eland

4. Founded in the 1920s and still a popular movement in Central Africa, what does 'Sape' stand for?
   A) Society of Artists and Extraordinary People
   B) Society of Ambience-Makers and Elegant People
   C) Society of Architects and Engineers

5. The name Gabon comes from a Portuguese word meaning what?
   A) Hat B) Blanket C) Cloak

6. Botswana is Africa's largest producer of which gemstones?
   A) Rubies B) Sapphires C) Diamonds

7. More than 80% of mountainous Lesotho is located at least 1800m (5900ft) above sea level, earning it what nickname?
   A) The Kingdom of Heaven
   B) The Kingdom of the Birds
   C) The Kingdom of the Sky

8. Which of the following statements about the Namib Desert is true?
   A) It's the world's largest desert
   B) It's the world's hottest desert
   C) It's the world's oldest desert

9. In what country would you find Sibebe, Africa's largest rock monolith (and the second largest in the world after Uluru)?
   A) Eswatini B) Mozambique C) Malawi

10. Mozambique is one of only two countries to feature what object on its flag?
    A) A hammer B) A firearm C) A sinking ship

11. What is the capital of Angola?
    A) Luanda B) Harare C) Mombasa

12. Which of these statements about Lake Malawi is true?
    A) It's the deepest lake in Africa
    B) It is the second largest lake in the world
    C) It is home to more fish species than any other lake in the world

13. What is the national bird of Namibia, Zimbabwe and Zambia?
    A) African grey parrot B) African fish eagle C) Common ostrich

14. Zimbabwe has 16 official languages. Which is the most widely spoken?
    A) Shona B) Ndebele C) English

15. South Africa is home to what percentage of the world's bird, fish and plant species?
    A) 2% B) 10% C) 40%

16. How long is the Congo, Africa's second-longest river?
    A) 3700km (2300 mi) B) 4700km (2900 mi) C) 5700km (3500 mi)

17. Virunga National Park in the Democratic Republic of Congo is Africa's oldest national park. True or false?

18. Around a third of the world's population of which animal lays its eggs in Gabon's Mayumba National Park each year?
    A) Wandering albatross B) Leatherback turtle C) Gaboon viper

19. Botswana's flag doesn't feature the Pan-African colours of red, green and yellow, but what colours instead?
    A) Blue, white, black B) Blue, orange, black C) Blue and black

20. In which country are the Kalandula Falls, one of Africa's largest falls?
    A) Botswana B) Malawi C) Angola

Quiz 53 **Monuments and Architecture**

1. At 182m (597ft) high, the Statue of Unity in India is the world's tallest statue. Which Indian statesperson does it depict?
    A) Vallabhbhai Patel B) Jawaharlal Nehru C) Mahatma Gandhi

2. How long did Paris' Arc de Triomphe take to build?
    A) Ten years B) Twenty years C) Thirty years

3. Excluding pedestals, what is the world's tallest statue of a woman?
    A) The Statue of Liberty, USA
    B) The Motherland Calls, Russia
    C) Monumento a la Virgen de la Paz, Venezuela

4. The Albert Memorial in London commemorates the death of the husband of which British monarch?
    A) Queen Anne B) Queen Victoria C) Queen Elizabeth II

5. Can you identify the building from the following description?
    Home to Europe's largest modern art museum, this Parisian building opened in 1977 and is named after a former French president.

6. In which Indian city is the flower-shaped Lotus Temple located ?
    A) Mumbai B) Delhi C) Agra

7. Which architect designed China's Guangzhou Opera House?
    A) Zaha Hadid B) Walter Gropius C) Norman Foster

8. Frank Lloyd Wright was associated with what style of architecture, inspired by the flat lands of the American midwest?
    A) Homestead School B) Great Plains School C) Prairie School

9. The Christ the Redeemer statue in Rio de Janeiro, Brazil was created by a Brazilian engineer and a sculptor from which country?
    A) Brazil B) France C) USA

10. In which New Zealand city would you find a statue of Pania, a figure from Māori mythology?
    A) Christchurch B) Hamilton C) Napier

- Landmarks & Buildings -

11. What is unusual about the location of Las Lajas Shrine, a Gothic-style church in Colombia?
A) It was built on top of a mountain
B) It was built inside a canyon
C) It was built on the edge of a waterfall

12. The Cenotaph, the UK's national war memorial, was designed by which architect?
A) Joseph Paxton B) George Gilbert Scott C) Edwin Lutyens

13. In what Canadian city would you find a geodesic dome called the Biosphere, containing a museum on the environment?
A) Montreal B) Vancouver C) Toronto

14. In which German city was the Bauhaus movement started?
A) Berlin B) Munich C) Weimar

15. In what city is the Taj Mahal located?
A) Chennai B) Kolkata C) Agra

16. The tallest statue on the African continent, the 49m (161ft) tall African Renaissance Monument towers above which capital city?
A) Dakar, Senegal B) Nairobi, Kenya C) Cairo, Egypt

17. Under construction since 1948, which Oglala Lakota warrior is being immortalised in a monument carved into Thunder Mountain in South Dakota, USA?
A) Kicking Bear B) Crazy Horse C) Flying Hawk

18. The Harpa concert hall opened in what European capital in 2011?
A) Reykjavík, Iceland B) Berlin, Germany C) Madrid Spain

19. Rome's famous amphitheatre, the Colosseum, was built when?
A) 2nd century BCE B) 1st century CE C) 10th century CE

20. Famed for its coloured glass, the Nasir al-Mulk Mosque in Iran is also known as what?
A) The Blue Mosque B) The Green Mosque C) The Pink Mosque

Quiz 54 **New York**

1. What was New York called before 1664?
    A) New London B) New Amsterdam C) New Paris

2. How many boroughs make up New York City?
    A) Five B) Ten C) Fifteen

3. In what year was the New York City Marathon first run?
    A) 1960 B) 1970 C) 1980

4. Established by Alexander Hamilton, which New York newspaper is the country's longest running daily newspaper?

5. Which theatre, named after an American composer, has been home to the hit musical *Wicked* since 2003?
    A) The Brooks Atkinson Theatre
    B) The Gershwin Theatre
    C) The Minskoff Theatre

6. 90 Bedford Street in New York's West Village is better known as what?
    A) The apartment block in *Friends*
    B) The setting for *Rosemary's Baby*
    C) Holly Golightly's home in *Breakfast at Tiffany's*

7. The Statue of Liberty was gifted to America by which nation?
    A) UK B) France C) The Netherlands

8. The borough of Queens was named after which English queen?
    A) Elizabeth I B) Mary of Modena C) Catherine of Braganza

9. The spire at the top of the Empire State Building was originally intended as a what?
    A) Hotel B) Climbing frame for gorillas C) Landing dock for airships

10. Which famous department store would you find on Herald Square in Manhattan?
    A) Macy's B) Bloomingdale's C) Saks

11. How long is Central Park?
    A) 1km (0.5 miles) B) 2km (1.2 miles) C) 4km (2.5 miles)

12. JFK and LaGuardia airports are both found in which borough?
    A) Manhattan B) Queens C) The Bronx

13. Which of these New York art museums is the largest?
    A) The Met B) The Guggenheim C) MoMA

14. What is the name of this building?

15. How many people pass through Grand Central Terminal each day?
    A) 7500 B) 75,000 C) 750,000

16. Which of the following sports would you expect to see being
    played at Madison Square Garden?
    A) American football B) Basketball C) Baseball

17. Which Ivy League university is located in Upper Manhattan?
    A) Columbia B) NYU C) Harvard

18. What is the name of New York's river?

19. The three main ingredients of a Manhattan cocktail are whisky,
    bitters and what else?
    A) Vermouth B) Ginger ale C) Lime juice

20. What is the name of the free ferry service that runs across New
    York Harbor 24 hours a day?

Quiz 55 **Natural Wonders**

1. One of the largest wetlands in the Mediterranean, the Camargue in France is famous for its population of what animal?
   A) River otters B) White horses C) Sea eagles

2. Containing a stone forest of stalactites and stalagmites, Zhijin Cave is the largest cave in China. How long is it?
   A) 2km (1.2 miles) B) 12km (7.5 miles) C) 20km (12 miles)

3. The cave also contains the world's tallest stalagmite? How tall is it?
   A) 10m (33ft) B) 35m (115ft) C) 70m (230ft)

4. How much of the world's land area is covered by grasslands?
   A) 10–20% B) 20–40% C) 40–60%

5. Approximately how much of the African continent is covered by tropical grassland, or savanna?
   A) 10% B) 25% C) 50%

6. Which of the these statements about the lake known as Waimangu Cauldron in New Zealand is true?
   A) It's the oldest lake in the world
   B) It's the largest hot spring in the world
   C) It's the deepest lake in the world

7. The Danube Delta, situated in Romania and Ukraine, is home to Europe's largest colony of which bird?
   A) Penguins B) Pelicans C) Flamingos

8. In what country is the tallest mountain in Europe?
   A) Russia B) Switzerland C) Germany

9. How many hot springs are there in Iceland?
   A) 15 B) 30 C) 45

10. The Okavango Delta, a vast wetland and wildlife haven, lies in which African country?
    A) Kenya B) Botswana C) Cameroon

- The Natural World -

11. One of the largest cave systems in Europe, the Frasassi Caves are located in which country?
    A) Austria B) Italy C) Switzerland

12. Can you identify the natural wonder from the description?
    A vast region of subtropical wetlands in the USA, it is the only place where the American crocodile and American alligator co-exist.

13. Native to the Eurasian steppe, what type of animal is the critically endangered saiga?
    A) A wild pony B) A mountain goat C) An antelope

14. What is the name of the tree common to African savanna regions that provides an important food source for giraffes?
    A) Acacia B) Baobab C) Fever tree

15. A UNESCO World Heritage Site, the Mesopotamian Marshes lie across the border of southern Iraq and which other country?
    A) Iran B) Syria C) Turkey

16. Uluru, Australia's most iconic landmark, is formed of what rock?
    A) Limestone B) Sandstone C) Granite

17. Native to the grasslands of North America, what type of mammal is a prairie dog?
    A) A rodent B) A dog C) A cat

18. The word 'prairie', used to describe grassland habitats in North America, comes from an old French word meaning what?
    A) Tall grass B) Flat land C) Meadow

19. The vast area of lowlands known as the Pampas are found predominantly in what South American country?
    A) Uruguay B) Brazil C) Argentina

20. What is the world's largest freshwater wetland?
    A) The Everglades, North America
    B) The Pantanal, South America
    C) The Sudd, Africa

Quiz 56 **General Travel Knowledge**

1. What was the name of the ship that blocked the Suez Canal for six days in March 2021?
    A) *Ever Forward* B) *Ever Given* C) *Evergreen*

2. Venice's famous *Ponte dei Sospiri* is a 17th-century bridge linking the city's main governmental palace with its prison. What does *Ponte dei Sospiri* mean?
    A) Bridge of Secrets B) Bridge of Suspicion C) Bridge of Sighs

3. Salt Lake City is the capital of which US state? And, for a bonus point, in which year did it host the Winter Olympics?

4. Native to Argentina, the smallest species of armadillo is known as the green goblin armadillo. True or false?

5. In Norway, *lutefisk* – a dish made of white fish that's been dried, pickled in lye and then steamed – is traditionally eaten at what time of year?
    A) Constitution Day B) Easter C) Christmas

6. Bubble tea originated in which Southeast Asian country?
    A) Taiwan B) Cambodia C) Thailand

7. The Netherlands national soccer teams play in what colour shirts?
    A) Red B) Orange C) Green

8. The orangutan is found living in the wild on just two Southeast Asian islands. Sumatra is one. What is the other?

9. What is the name of the commune and 'Freetown' that was founded in 1971 in the centre of Copenhagen and is still inhabited by around 1,000 people?
    A) Christiania B) Alexandra C) Victoriana

10. The Church of Our Lady Mary of Zion in Axum, Ethiopia, claims to hold which religious object?
    A) The Ark of the Covenant B) The Holy Grail C) The True Cross

11. In 1950, what two cities became the first in the world to be classed as megacities – cities with a population of over 10 million?
    A) London and Delhi
    B) New York and Tokyo
    C) Shanghai and Mexico City

12. Which of these languages spoken in the Nordic countries is *not* classed as a Nordic (or North Germanic) language?
    A) Swedish B) Icelandic C) Finnish

13. What is the capital of Papua New Guinea?

14. Who did Barack Obama succeed as President of the United States?

15. Which of these African rivers flows into the Atlantic Ocean?
    A) The Nile B) The Zambezi C) The Congo

16. The National University of San Marcos, the oldest continuously operating university in the Americas, is in what country?
    A) USA B) Peru C) Mexico

17. In what capital city would you find this government building, known locally as the 'Beehive'?
    A) Wellington, New Zealand B) Ottawa, Canada C) Rome, Italy

18. Who was the first president of Russia?

19. In what decade of the 20th century did Iran officially change its name to Persia?
    A) 1930s B) 1950s C) 1970s

20. By area, which country is bigger, England or Scotland?

Quiz 57 **Buses and Bikes**

1. With almost 200 million passengers every year, which Southeast Asian city has the world's largest and busiest bus network?
   A) Manila, Philippines B) Jakarta, Indonesia C) Bangkok, Thailand

2. With more than more than 421,000 electric buses circulating in its cities, which country has the biggest fleet of electric buses?
   A) USA B) China C) Russia

3. London buses are famously red. But why was this colour picked?
   A) To match the colour of the UK's post boxes
   B) So the buses could be seen more easily at night
   C) To stand out from competitors

4. What's the name of the iconic model of double-decker bus which operated in London between 1956 and 2005?
   A) Beefeater B) Routemaster C) Trafalgar

5. Which bus company connects all the countries in Central America, apart from Belize?
   A) Tica Bus B) Aztec Bus C) Plus Bux

6. Started in 1914, what is the USA's largest intercity bus service?
   A) Greyhound B) Amtrak C) Buffalo Buses

7. Buses make up what percentage of public transport in Indian cities?
   A) 25% B) 50% C) 90%

8. In which US city did Rosa Parks refuse to give up her seat on a bus, one of the major moments of the US civil rights movement?
   A) Montgomery B) Mobile C) Birmingham

9. Which Scandinavian city was the first capital in the world to have a bus service powered by 100% renewable energy?
   A) Stockholm, Sweden B) Oslo, Norway C) Helsinki, Norway

10. Tap taps are brightly coloured buses in which Caribbean country?
    A) Jamaica B) Haiti C) Cuba

11. Annie Cohen Kopchovsky, also known as Annie Londonderry, famously achieved which cycling feat?
    A) She was the first woman to win an Olympic gold medal in cycling
    B) She was the first woman to ride a bicycle around the world
    C) She was the first woman to compete in the Tour de France

12. What colour jersey does the leader of the Tour de France wear?
    A) Blue B) Red C) Yellow

13. Which country is the largest exporter of bikes in the world?
    A) China B) Taiwan C) The Netherlands

14. What is New York's official bike-sharing scheme called?
    A) NYCycle B) Citi Bike C) Big Apple Bikes

15. Only three countries in the world have laws that enforce the wearing of bike helmets for all ages. Australia and New Zealand are two – can you name the third?
    A) Sweden B) China C) Argentina

16. What Asian city is the 'rickshaw capital of the world' with more than a million cycle taxis found on its streets?
    A) Dhaka, Bangladesh B) Hanoi, Vietnam C) Beijing, China

17. Often called the most bike-friendly city in the world, what is the extent of the Danish capital Copenhagen's cycle lanes?
    A) 200km (125 mi) B) 400km (250 mi) C) 600km (370 mi)

18. Which of the following is a genuine rule on Thailand's roads?
    A) You must have a driver's licence to ride a bicycle
    B) You cannot ride a bike shirtless
    C) You have to have at least six lights on your bike

19. What endurance event sees cyclists race from the west coast to the east coast of America?
    A) Tour de America B) Race Across America C) Bike USA

20. What is the men's world record for cycling around the world?
    A) 25 days B) 78 days C) 101 days

Quiz 58 **China**

1. What is the capital of China?

2. How many signs make up the Chinese Zodiac?

3. When does Chinese New Year begin?
   A) 1 January B) 28 February C) Between 21 January and 20 February

4. How many days do the festivities last?
   A) 10 days B) 15 days C) 20 days

5. One of the country's most recognizable landmarks, what is the Forbidden City?
   A) China's parliament building
   B) The former imperial palace – now a museum
   C) A luxury hotel

6. The four great inventions of ancient China were paper making, printing, gunpowder and what else?

7. How many time zones are there across China?
   A) One B) Two C) Four

8. Roughly, how long is the Great Wall of China?
   A) 8800km (5500 miles)
   B) 21,200km (13,200 miles)
   C) 51,300km (31,900 miles)

9. The mortar used to build sections of the Great Wall of China contained what?
   A) Bamboo leaves B) Sticky rice C) Tea leaves

10. What colour is traditionally worn by Chinese brides on their wedding day?
    A) White B) Black C) Red

11. Mount Everest lies across China's border with which country?

12. Built in the third century BCE, when was the Terracotta Army rediscovered?
    A) 13th century B) 1865 C) 1974

13. The Yangtze is number one, but what is the second longest river in China?
    A) Yellow River B) Heilongjiang C) Pearl River

14. What is unusual about black snub-nosed monkeys, found only in China's Yunnan province?
    A) They are the largest species of monkey in the world
    B) They live at the highest altitude of any (non-human) primate
    C) They only come down to the ground once a week to poo

15. What is *Tangyuan*, a dessert that is traditionally eaten on the final day of Chinese New Year celebrations?
    A) Mooncake B) Water chestnut cake C) Glutinous rice balls

16. Which of these statements about Shanghai's metro system is true?
    A) It is the smallest in the world by route length
    B) It is the largest in the world by route length
    C) It has the largest number of stations in the world

17. What is the tallest building in China?
    A) Shanghai Tower
    B) Ping An Finance Centre, Shenzhen
    C) China Zun, Beijing

18. How long do giant pandas spend eating bamboo each day?
    A) 1–4 hours B) 5–9 hours C) 10–16 hours

19. In imperial China, the emperor wore robes with embroidered dragons. What creatures featured on the empress's robes?
    A) Unicorns B) Phoenixes C) Cranes

20. How many stars are there on the Chinese flag?
    A) Four B) Five C) Six

Quiz 59 **South Asia**

1. Which is the only one of these cities that the River Ganges flows through?
    A) Mumbai B) Delhi C) Varanasi

2. What is the capital of Pakistan?

3. Which Hindu festival is also known as the Festival of Spring or the Festival of Colours?
    A) Diwali B) Holi C) Shivaratri

4. What is the national tree of India?
    A) Teak tree B) Banyan tree C) Mango tree

5. Bangladesh's calendar year is traditionally divided into how many seasons?
    A) Two B) Four C) Six

6. What are the two main religions of Nepal?
    A) Hinduism and Buddhism
    B) Hinduism and Islam
    C) Hinduism and Sikhism

7. The highest mountain in the world, Mount Everest is called *Sagarmatha* in Sanskrit and Nepali – which translates as what?
    A) Giant peak B) Peak of heaven C) Peak 15

8. Which of the following facts about Bhutan is false?
    A) Its name translates as 'Land of the Thunder Dragon'
    B) It is polite in Bhutan to refuse food when it is offered to you
    C) It is a largely Hindu nation

9. Which national park in Rajasthan, India, is particularly famous for its population of Bengal tigers?
    A) Silent Valley National Park
    B) Manas National Park
    C) Ranthambore National Park

10. Which Pakistani activist won the Nobel Peace Prize in 2014?
    A) Malala Yousafzai B) Kailash Satyarthi C) Shirin Ebadi

11. What is the national animal of Bangladesh?
    A) The Sun bear B) The Bengal tiger C) The mongoose

12. How high above sea level is Nepal's capital city, Kathmandu?
    A) 1000m (3300ft) B) 1300m (4300ft) C) 2300m (7500ft)

13. Gangkhar Puensum, a mountain in Bhutan, is what?
    A) The world's highest unclimbed mountain
    B) The smallest peak in the Himalayas
    C) The only mountain in the world with five peaks

14. What is the commercial capital of Sri Lanka
    A) Colombo B) Kandy C) Sri Jayawardenepura Kotte

15. Which 1997 Booker-Prize-winning novel set in Kerala, India,
    focuses on the lives of two twins?
    A) *The White Tiger* B) *The God of Small Things* C) *Untouchable*

16. Located in Pakistan, what is the world's second-highest mountain?
    A) C1 B) K2 C) R3

17. Which two countries border Bangladesh?
    A) India and China B) India and Nepal C) India and Myanmar

18. What is the name of the square in the heart of historic Kathmandu
    that is surrounded by palaces and temples?
    A) Durbar Square B) St Mark's Square C) Kathmandu Square

19. What is the longest and largest river in Pakistan?
    A) Indus B) Ganges C) Euphrates

20. What is Sri Lanka's currency?
    A) Sri Lankan rupee B) Sri Lankan yuan C) Sri Lankan baht

Quiz 60 **Food and Drink**

1. What is the main ingredient of the Japanese alcoholic drink *sake*?
   A) Fermented fish B) Fermented rice C) Fermented wasabi

2. The national dish of Iceland, *hákarl* is fermented what?
   A) Shark B) Puffin C) Narwhal

3. If you were to order *cuy* in Peru, what would you be served?
   A) Llama B) Guinea Pig C) Capybara

4. What percentage of the world's maple syrup comes from Canada?
   A) 31% B) 51% C) 71%

5. Parmesan is an Italian hard cheese made from the milk of which animal?
   A) Cow B) Sheep C) Goat

6. One of the world's most expensive fruits is the Japanese Yubari King. In 2019, a pair sold for a record-breaking 5 million yen. What type of fruit is it?
   A) Apple B) Pear C) Melon

7. In Cornwall, England, a local delicacy is stargazey pie. What is it?
   A) A Cornish pasty baked in the shape of a star
   B) A baked fish pie with fish heads poking out of the crust
   C) A blackbird pie in which all the beaks point upwards

8. In the Indian dish *saag aloo*, what does the '*aloo*' refer to?
   A) Spinach B) Potato C) Tomato

9. Which French city is at the centre of the Champagne wine region?
   A) Paris B) Lyon C) Reims

10. Bunny chow is a popular South African fast food. Which of these descriptions best matches it?
    A) A thick soup made from antelope meat
    B) A spicy curry served in a hollowed-out loaf of bread
    C) A pickled fish served with chopped vegetables and mustard

11. Which of these herbs is a key ingredient of the Middle-Eastern salad tabbouleh?
    A) Basil B) Parsley C) Mint

12. What drink is known as *caldo de cana* in Brazil, *asab* in Egypt and *minuman sari tebu* in Indonesia?
    A) Iced tea B) Sugarcane juice C) Mango juice

13. In which Indian state did the spicy curry dish vindaloo originate?
    A) Kerala B) Punjab C) Goa

14. A classic North American grilled sandwich, the Reuben consists of which of the following ingredients:
    A) Corned beef, Swiss cheese, sauerkraut, dressing and rye bread
    B) Pepperoni, Swiss cheese, lettuce and rye bread
    C) Baloney, Swiss cheese, dressing and sourdough bread

15. Popular in Germany, what type of food is *spaetzle*?
    A) Bagels B) Potato pies C) Egg noodle dumplings

16. One of the most popular desserts in Thailand is a sticky rice dish made with fresh what?
    A) Pineapple B) Mango C) Dragon fruit

17. What classic Mexican street food consists of grilled corn on the cob covered in a spicy and creamy sauce?
    A) Taco B) Churro C) Elote

18. Hoppers are a popular breakfast dish in Sri Lanka. What is a hopper?
    A) A cured fish B) A bowl-shaped pancake C) A fried grasshopper

19. Which of these is not an Australian beer?
    A) Victoria Bitter B) Tooheys C) Speights

20. At Thanksgiving in the USA, what might be baked on top of a sweet potato casserole?
    A) Marshmallows B) Peanut butter C) Turkey

Quiz 61 **Around the World in 25 Journeys**

1. Covering nearly 776 sq (300 sq miles), which of these is the world's largest airport?
    A) Cairo International Airport, Egypt
    B) King Fahd International Airport, Saudi Arabia
    C) Beijing Daxing International Airport, China

2. The world's longest bus route, the Transoceánica shuttles passengers 6000km (3700 miles) between cities on either side of which continent?

3. The narrow gauge railway that chugs up into the Himalayas of West Bengal, India, shares its name with which type of tea?
    A) Darjeeling B) Assam C) Oolong

4. Traditionally, what colour are the taxis in New York?

5. And what colour are the taxis in London?

6. The boats used by Vikings on their journeys of plunder and conquest across Europe were known as what?

7. Common to the cities of East Africa, what is a *boda boda*?
    A) An open-back bus B) A motorcycle taxi C) A rope ferry

8. In what country was the hot-air balloon invented?

9. The intercity bus service founded in the USA in 1914 is named after which animal?

10. On the London Underground map, which line is coloured black?
    A) Piccadilly B) Jubilee C) Northern

11. What country has more bicycles per person than any other?
    A) China B) Costa Rica C) The Netherlands

12. In what European country would you find airports with these three codes: CGN, FRA, and BER?

13. A junk is a type of ship from which country?

14. If you're riding the train known as the Ghan, what country are you travelling across?
    A) Afghanistan B) Ghana C) Australia

15. In what country is the luxury car firm Bugatti Automobiles based?
    A) Italy B) Germany C) France

16. A popular form of transport in the Philippines, what is a *jeepney*?
    A) A bus B) A train C) A ferry

17. Used to zip between Greek Islands, the super-fast boats known as hydrofoils have been given which local nickname?
    A) Flying dolphins B) Jumping sharks C) Rushing whales

18. Russia's Lena River is used as an ice road in winter. True or false?

19. Named after its German inventor, what was the dominant form of airship in the early 20th century?

20. In the 2004 film, *The Terminal*, Tom Hanks stars as a man stuck in which US airport?
    A) JFK, New York B) Los Angeles International C) Chicago O'Hare

21. Voted the greatest British painting in a BBC poll, *The Fighting Temeraire* by J.M.W. Turner features what type of vehicle?

22. What is the name of the section of an airport where aircraft board, unload and refuel?
    A) Apron B) Bib C) Napkin

23. In what year was the wreck of the *Titanic* discovered?
    A) 1945 B) 1965 C) 1985

24. Used in much of East Africa, what sort of vehicle is a dhow?
    A) A boat B) A train C) A truck

25. The Flying Doctor is an aerial medical service in which country?

Quiz 62 **The UK**

1. Both Great Britain and the United Kingdom are made up of three countries. True or false?

2. What is the UK's highest mountain?
    A) Ben Nevis **B)** Snowdon **C)** Scafell Pike

3. What is the UK's longest river?
    A) Severn **B)** Thames **C)** Trent

4. What is the second largest city in the UK?
    A) Edinburgh, Scotland **B)** Birmingham, England **C)** Cardiff, Wales

5. The Norfolk Broads in the east of England are characterised by what sort of landscape?
    A) White cliffs **B)** Beaches **C)** Inland waterways

6. The first reports of a monster lurking in Loch Ness in Scotland date back to which century?
    A) 6th century **B)** 16th century **C)** 20th century

7. Which British author is believed to be the best-selling female author of all time?
    A) Agatha Christie **B)** Barbara Cartland **C)** J K Rowling

8. The counties that surround London are known as the 'home counties'. Which of these is not a home country?
    A) Surrey **B)** Oxfordshire **C)** Gloucestershire

9. In which English county can you find the ancient Neolithic stone circle of Stonehenge?
    A) Somerset **B)** Hampshire **C)** Wiltshire

10. Roughly how old is Stonehenge?
    A) 2000 years old **B)** 5000 years old **C)** 10,000 years old

11. The Welsh flag features a dragon at its centre. What colour is it?
    A) Red **B)** Green **C)** White

12. What is the name of the natural feature on the coast of Northern Ireland featuring 40,000 interlinking, hexagonal basalt columns?
    A) The Devil's Causeway
    B) The Giant's Causeway
    C) The Mariner's Causeway

13. A 'Munro' is a Scottish mountain above what height?
    A) 300ft (91m) B) 3000ft (914m) C) 13,000ft (3962m)

14. What is the name of this iconic statue, erected in 1998?

15. The Black Country, so named because of the soot that used to fill the air during the Industrial Revolution, is a region in which part of the UK?
    A) Midlands, England B) Northern Ireland C) Northeast Scotland

16. What prime minister was in power during the Falklands War of 1982?
    A) Edward Heath B) Margaret Thatcher C) Tony Blair

17. In which English city is the TV series *Peaky Blinders* set?
    A) Birmingham B) Manchester C) Liverpool

18. In what year was Queen Elizabeth II born?
    A) 1916 B) 1926 C) 1936

19. And in what year did she ascend to the throne?
    A) 1952 B) 1953 C) 1954

20. A traditional Scottish item, what is a sporran?
    A) A kilt pouch B) A small bottle of whisky C) A walking stick

Quiz 63 **World Heritage Sites**

1. UNESCO, the international body charged with identifying and preserving World Heritage Sites, was founded in what year?
   A) 1925 B) 1945 C) 1985

2. In what city are UNESCO's headquarters?
   A) New York, USA B) Paris, France C) Zurich, Switzerland

3. Which World Heritage Site is considered by some experts to be the oldest continuously occupied city in the world?
   A) Jerusalem, Israel B) Athens, Greece C) Damascus, Syria

4. What country has the greatest number of World Heritage Sites?
   A) Mexico B) Italy C) Russia

5. What country has the largest area given over to World Heritage Sites?
   A) USA B) Canada C) Australia

6. Which British city was stripped of its World Heritage status in 2021?
   A) Bath B) Liverpool C) Edinburgh

7. In total, how many sites have been stripped of their World Heritage status?
   A) Three B) Fourteen C) Twenty

8. Which is the world's least populous city that is listed as a World Hertage Site?
   A) Monaco B) Vatican City C) Hong Kong, China

9. Which of these Australian sites is not on the World Heritage List?
   A) Great Barrier Reef
   B) Sydney Harbour Bridge
   C) Sydney Opera House

10. Which of these African countries has the largest number of World Heritage Sites?
    A) Cameroon B) Egypt C) Ethiopia

11. Which country has more World Heritage Sites, China or France?

12. What World Heritage Site occupies a tidal island off the coast of Normandy, France?
   A) Carcassone B) Mont-St-Michel C) Grand Île de Strasbourg

13. The US Declaration of Independence was signed in what World Heritage Site?
   A) Independence Hall, Philadelphia
   B) The Capitol Building, Washington DC
   C) Monticello, Virginia

14. Which of these sites gained World Heritage status most recently?
   A) Historic Centre of Kraków, Poland
   B) Yellowstone National Park, USA
   C) Vatican City

15. Which World Heritage cathedral remained standing despite receiving 14 direct hits by aerial bombs in the Second World War?
   A) Cologne, Germany B) Canterbury, UK C) Notre-Dame, France

16. The Struve Geodetic Arc, a 19th-century chain of triangulation points for measuring the size of the Earth, is a World Heritage Site spanning several European countries. How many exactly?
   A) Six B) Ten C) Twenty

17. The ruins of the ancient city of Troy are in which country?
   A) Turkey B) Greece C) Italy

18. Which South American archipelago has been awarded World Heritage Status in honour of its diverse ecosystem?

19. The island of Skellig Michael of the coast of Ireland is featured in what movie series?
   A) The Hobbit B) Star Wars C) The Matrix

20. How many World Heritage Sites does the UK have?
   A) Three B) Twenty Three C) Thirty Three

Quiz 64 **The Cities of Italy**

1. According to legend, in what year was Rome founded?
   A) 753 BCE B) 146 BCE C) 27 BCE

2. On how many hills was the city built?
   A) Three B) Five C) Seven

3. At the heart of every Roman city, what was the forum?
   A) A public square B) Public baths C) A courthouse

4. The Renaissance artists Leonardo da Vinci and Botticelli were born in or in the outskirts of which city?
   A) Siena B) Florence C) Palermo

5. The city of Bologna is home to the world's oldest what?
   A) Restaurant B) University C) Hotel

6. Since repair work was completed in 2001, by how many degrees does the Leaning Tower of Pisa tilt over from the perpendicular?
   A) 4° B) 8° C) 14°

7. In what northern Italian city is William Shakespeare's play *Romeo and Juliet* set?
   A) Milan B) Verona C) Turin

8. Which Italian food staple did Naples give to the world?
   A) Lasagne B) Pizza C) Risotto

9. Milan is the capital of which Italian region?
   A) Tuscany B) Lombardy C) Piedmont

10. What is the name of the banking family that came to dominate the political life of Florence during the Renaissance?
    A) The Medici B) The Borgia C) The Sforza

11. In which city was explorer Christopher Columbus born, in 1451?
    A) Perugia B) Padua C) Genoa

12. In what year did Rome host the Summer Olympic Games?
    A) 1932 B) 1960 C) 1976

13. In what year did Turin host the Winter Olympic Games?
    A) 1980 B) 1994 C) 2006

14. By population, what is the largest city in Sicily?
    A) Palermo B) Syracuse C) Catania

15. What river flows through Rome?

16. These are the ruins of which Roman city?
    A) Rome B) Pompeii C) Verona

17. What was the first capital of the newly united Italy in 1861?
    A) Turin B) Florence C) Rome

18. What is the name of the 1960 film directed by Federico Fellini
    that features a famous scene in which Anita Ekberg and Marcello
    Mastroianni cavort in Rome's Trevi Fountain?

19. If you wanted to see Leonardo da Vinci's *The Last Supper*, what
    Italian city would you need to visit?
    A) Florence B) Milan C) Naples

20. What's the name of the famous horse race that's been held in
    Siena's central square since the Middle Ages?

Quiz 65 **Volcanoes**

1. Which country has the largest number of active volcanoes?
   A) Indonesia B) USA C) Russia

2. Of the four main types of lava: a'a, pāhoehoe, blocky and pillow, what is the type that forms underwater?

3. The names for a'a and pāhoehoe lava are derived from which language?
   A) Indonesian B) Hawaiian C) Arabic

4. What is a volcanic plug?
   A) A device used to prevent a volcanic eruption
   B) A hard magma formation that blocks a volcano's vent
   C) A small volcanic cone growing from the side of a main cone

5. The sport of volcano boarding involves being lowered into the mouth of an active volcano on a suspended platform. True or false?

6. In which year was Iceland's most recent volcanic eruption?
   A) 1963 B) 1996 C) 2021

7. Which of these is not an official term for a type of volcano?
   A) Cinder B) Ash C) Shield

8. What is the name of Ethiopia's highly volcanic region, famed for its multicoloured hot springs
   A) Dallol B) Pinatubo C) Bulusan

9. How many times has Mount Karthala in the Comoros erupted over the past 200 years?
   A) Two B) Five C) Twenty

10. What is the local nickname for the Mexican volcano Popocatépetl?
    A) Popso B) El Popo C) Popeye

11. In which ocean can you find the 40,000km (25,000-mile) line of volcanic activity known as the Ring of Fire?

12. Fonuafo'ou, an island that periodically disappears and reappears due to the activity of a submarine volcano, lies of the coast of which island nation?
A) Cuba B) Madagascar C) Tonga

13. Which of these is not a volcano?
A) Mount Fuji B) Mount Everest C) Mount Kilimanjaro

14. What is the definition of a volcanic hotspot?
A) A place where lava bursts straight through the Earth's crust rather than at a tectonic boundary
B) A place where lava comes into contact with freshwater, turning it instantly into steam
C) A type of enclosed volcanic chamber with no outlet where temperatures are over three times hotter than normal

15. What is the definition of a dormant volcano?
A) A volcano that erupts occasionally, but not seriously
B) A volcano that hasn't erupted in human recorded history
C) A volcano that it is known will never erupt again

16. What was the Icelandic volcano that blew enormous amounts of ash into the air in 2010, causing flight disruption around the world?
A) Snæfellsjökull B) Eyjafjallajökull C) Katla

17. Italy has three active volcanoes: Vesuvius, Etna and what other, located on an island just north of Sicily?

18. What is the name of the crater formed when a magma chamber collapses after a volcanic eruption?

19. Some people believe the dormant volcano Mount Ararat in Turkey to be the final resting place of what object from the Bible?
A) Noah's Ark B) The Ark of the Covenant C) The True Cross

20. The world's tallest mountain if measured from the seabed, Mauna Kea's name means what?
A) Giant God B) White Mountain C) Iceberg Rock

Quiz 66 **General Travel Knowledge**

1. In what country can you visit the Chocolate Hills, a range of rolling peaks topped with grass that turns brown in the dry season, hence the name?
   A) Sri Lanka B) The Philippines C) Laos

2. Which of these countries is not considered part of the Balkans?
   A) Serbia B) Montenegro C) Ukraine

3. By population, what is the largest city in South America?
   A) Bogotá, Colombia B) São Paulo, Brazil C) Santiago, Chile

4. Of Greece's 6000 plus islands, how many are inhabited (according to the Greek Tourist Board)?
   A) 27 B) 127 C) 227

5. Which of these countries is not landlocked?
   A) Afghanistan B) Bolivia C) Oman

6. The Whitsunday Islands are located just off the mainland of which country?
   A) Jamaica B) Australia C) Scotland

7. Which architect designed New York's Guggenheim Museum?
   A) Frank Gehry B) Frank Lloyd Wright C) Le Corbusier

8. What are the three Baltic states?

9. Kathmandu is the capital of which country?
   A) Nepal B) Bhutan C) Myanmar (Burma)

10. In which European country can you find Bohemian Switzerland National Park?
    A) Switzerland B) Germany C) Czech Republic

11. What African country has an 'Avenue of the Baobabs'?
    A) Kenya B) Botswana C) Madagascar

12. In what year did India and Pakistan gain independence from Britain?
A) 1947 B) 1957 C) 1967

13. What is the world's largest island?

14. What are the 'Fairy Chimneys' of Cappadocia in Turkey?
A) Unusual rock formations
B) Distinctively shaped fir trees
C) Columns from ancient Greek temples that have remained standing after the rest of the building has collapsed

15. The Grand Canyon is in which US state?
A) Texas B) California C) Arizona

16. What is the capital of Vietnam?
A) Ha Long Bay B) Hanoi C) Ho Chi Minh City

17. The dish known as *Dolma*, which is popular across the Balkans, Greece and the Middle East, consists of a savoury filling wrapped in what?
A) Vine leaves B) Wheat pancakes C) Fish skin

18. Two of these cities are in Australia and one is in New Zealand. Which one?
A) Cairns B) Dunedin C) Geelong

19. There's a statue of the J.M. Barrie character Peter Pan erected by the author, in which London park?
A) Kensington Gardens B) Kew Gardens C) Hampstead Heath

20. South Africa's Witwatersrand Basin is an underground geological formation that holds the world's largest known reserves of what precious commodity?
A) Gold B) Diamonds C) Platinum

Quiz 67 **Mexico**

1. What is the official language of Mexico?
   A) Spanish B) Mexican C) It doesn't have one

2. What is Mexico's currency?
   A) Mexican Dollar B) Mexican Peso C) Mexican Balboa

3. Which of these is not an ancient Mexican civilization?
   A) Olmec B) Toltec C) Inca

4. What is the name of the impact crater just off Mexico's coast caused by the asteroid that hit the Earth 66 million years ago, wiping out the dinosaurs?
   A) Tookoonooka B) Chicxulub C) Manicouagan

5. Which of these statements is correct?
   A) Mexico City's buildings are sinking
   B) Mexico City's buildings are rising up
   C) Mexico City's buildings are being dragged sideways

6. A Mexican delicacy, a quesadilla is a filled tortilla that is then...?
   A) Rolled into a cylindrical shape and eaten cold
   B) Folded in half and pan fried
   C) Covered in sauce and oven-baked

7. Mexico straddles how many tectonic plates?
   A) Three B) Five C) Seven

8. Which Mexican filmmaker directed *Pan's Labyrinth*, *Hellboy* and *The Shape of Water*?

9. What was the name of the Aztec capital over which the modern capital of Mexico City was built in the 16th century?
   A) Tenochtitlan B) Texcoco C) Chichén Itzá

10. What are the four US states that border Mexico to the north? You get a point for each.

11. What are the two Central American countries that border Mexico to the south? Again, you get a point for each.

12. Which Mexican resort has inspired songs by the Four Tops, Jason Derulo and Juan Gabriel?
A) Tulum B) Cancún C) Acapulco

13. How many time zones are there in Mexico?
A) Three B) Four C) Five

14. In which year was the artist Frida Kahlo born?
A) 1907 B) 1917 C) 1927

15. What is the name given to the genre of traditional Mexican music, featuring stringed instruments and trumpets, which is usually performed by strolling musicians?
A) Fado B) Mariachi C) Bluegrass

16. Which 2017 Disney Pixar feature film is set in Mexico?
A) *Luca* B) *Encanto* C) *Coco*

17. What is the main ingredient in the traditional Mexican breakfast, *huevos rancheros*?
A) Beans B) Chicken C) Eggs

18. What is the name of the peninsula in the country's southeast that partly separates the Gulf of Mexico from the Caribbean Sea?
A) Baja California B) Yucatán C) Kenai

19. In what year did Mexico City host the Summer Olympic Games?
A) 1968 B) 1984 C) 2008

20. Mexico is one of five countries to have hosted the men's football World Cup twice, once in 1970 and then again when?
A) 1978 B) 1986 C) 1994

Quiz 68 **Central and Eastern Europe**

1. Which country uses the forint as its currency?
   A) Romania B) Ukraine C) Hungary

2. What is the mountain range that runs north to south through central Russia and acts as an unofficial diving line between Europe and Asia?
   A) The Caucasus B) The Urals C) The Carpathians

3. Which Polish-born scientist was the first person to win two Nobel Prizes? For two extra points, in what disciplines?

4. Which East European structure is the world's heaviest building, weighing around 4 million tonnes (4.1 million tons)?
   A) Palace of the Parliament, Bucharest, Romania
   B) St Basil's Cathedral, Moscow, Russia
   C) Hungarian Parliament Building, Budapest, Hungary

5. What is the main ingredient in the popular East European sour soup, *borscht*?
   A) Smoked fish B) Beetroot C) Sauerkraut

6. What was the deadly nickname of the 15th-century Romanian ruler, Vlad Dracula, the supposed inspiration for Count Dracula?

7. What is the capital of the Croatia?

8. The flag of which East European country features a band of blue above a band of yellow?

9. How many countries does the Danube River flow through?
   A) Five B) Ten C) Fifteen

10. A traditional dish in Moldova, what is *mămăligă*?
    A) Maize porridge B) Beef stew C) Saffron-flavored ice cream

11. What is the name of the establishment in Vienna where Lipzanner horses are trained to perform dressage?

12. Following a devastating accident in 1986, the area around the Chernobyl Nuclear Power Plant in Ukraine is estimated to remain highly radioactive for how long?
    A) 200 years B) 2000 years C) 20,000 years

13. Which nation consumes more beer per person than anywhere else in the world?
    A) Czech Republic B) Hungary C) Poland

14. Which Central European capital city is the only one in the world to border two other countries?
    A) Bucharest, Romania
    B) Skopje, North Macedonia
    C) Bratislava, Slovakia

15. Popular treats across Central and Eastern Europe, what are *pierogi*?
    A) Pickled gherkins B) Dumplings C) Blood sausages

16. In what year did Czechoslovakia split into two new nations: the Czech Republic and Slovakia?
    A) 1983 B) 1993 C) 2003

17. What is Poland's second largest city, after Warsaw?
    A) Kraków B) Gdańsk C) Poznań

18. Ernő Rubik, the creator of the fiendishly difficult eponymous puzzle the Rubik's Cube, is from what country?
    A) Croatia B) Austria C) Hungary

19. What is the name of the modernist building in Prague, Czech Republic, that resembles a pair of intertwined dancers?
    A) The Dancing House
    B) The Tango Tenement
    C) The Gyratoscope

20. Prior to its re-emergence in 1918, for how long had Poland not existed as an independent country?
    A) 23 years B) 73 years C) 123 years

 Score

Quiz 69 **Money and Currencies**

1. According to the United Nations, how many official currencies are there in the world?
   A) 80 B) 180 C) 800

2. Across the world, who is the most commonly printed figure on bank notes?
   A) Queen Elizabeth II B) George Washington C) Nelson Mandela

3. Every year, more new Monopoly money is printed than real new money in the USA. True or false?

4. What is the oldest currency still in use today?
   A) Turkish lira B) British pound sterling C) Indian rupee

5. The first coins were issued in the ancient kingdom of Lydia in what is now modern Turkey in what century?
   A) 7th century BCE B) 1st century BCE C) 2nd century CE

6. Those first coins were made of a naturally occurring alloy of gold and silver known as what?
   A) Silvergold B) Croesium C) Electrum

7. Whale teeth used to be used as money in which island country?
   A) Barbados B) Fiji C) Indonesia

8. In what decade of the 20th century was the credit card created by the company Diners Club?
   A) 1920s B) 1950s C) 1970s

9. Which technology company invented the magnetic strip that has made modern bank cards possible?
   A) IBM B) Apple C) Microsoft

10. Which country was the first to use paper money?
    A) India B) Japan C) China

11. The bridges depicted on the back of Euro notes do not represent real structures. True or false?

12. What was the first cryptocurrrency?
    A) Dogecoin B) Bitcoin C) Namecoin

13. As well as being a founding father of the USA, Benjamin Franklin was also in charge of printing the currency for Pennsylvania and New Jersey. In order to deter counterfeiters, which word did he deliberately misspell on dollar bills?
    A) Mississippi B) Pennsylvania C) Jersey

14. Which of the following is not a real currency?
    A) Birr B) Dong C) Pico

15. What is the study or collection of money known as?
    A) Numerology B) Numismatics C) Coinology

16. Which country uses the lempira as its currency?
    A) Honduras B) Ghana C) India

17. In what European country will having 100 eyrir get you 1 krona?
    A) Denmark B) Norway C) Iceland

18. What was Austria's currency before the Euro?
    A) The schilling B) The mark C) The guilder

19. Which country's currency is the tögrög?
    A) Mongolia B) Nepal C) Georgia

20. There are two African currencies known as the CFA Franc, which are used by multiple countries. One is the Central African CFA Franc. What is the other?
    A) East African CFA Franc
    B) West African CFA Franc
    C) North African CFA Franc

Quiz 70 **What in the World?**

Can you name the country in each of the 20 circled areas
from the three available options?

1. A) Canada B) Greenland C) USA
2. A) Mexico B) USA C) Colombia
3. A) Canada B) Greenland C) USA
4. A) Ecuador B) Peru C) Chile
5. A) Brazil B) Suriname C) Venezuela

6. A) Ghana B) Côte d'Ivoire C) Egypt
7. A) Scotland B) England C) Wales
8. A) Portugal B) Spain C) Italy
9. A) Poland B) Germany C) France
10. A) Angola B) Namibia C) Kenya

11. A) Sweden B) Finland C) Latvia
12. A) Turkey B) Greece C) Azerbaijan
13. A) Ethiopia B) Tanzania C) Gabon
14. A) UAE B) Oman C) Iraq
15. A) India B) Bahrain C) Sri Lanka

16. A) Russia B) Mongolia C) Japan
17. A) Taiwan B) China C) Cambodia
18. A) Philippines B) Malaysia C) Japan
19. A) Papua New Guinea B) Laos C) Fiji
20. A) Australia B) New Zealand C) Nauru

Quiz 71 **General Travel Knowledge**

1. What is the world's most northerly capital city?
   A) Oslo, Norway B) Ottawa, Canada C) Reykjavík, Iceland

2. What is the world's highest capital city?
   A) La Paz, Bolivia B) Quito, Ecuador C) Thimphu, Bhutan

3. What river runs through the centre of Paris?
   A) The Seine B) The Rhine C) The Loire

4. What is the only one of the four Grand Slam tennis events to be played on grass?
   A) Australian Open B) Wimbledon C) French Open

5. What is the word's shallowest sea with a maximum depth of just 14m (46ft)?
   A) The Caribbean Sea B) The Sea of Azov C) The Coral Sea

6. What is Croatia's currency?
   A) The kuna B) The euro C) The lek

7. What sport do the Boston Bruins play?
   A) Baseball B) Basketball C) Ice hockey

8. The distinctive looking Guggenheim Museum Bilbao in Spain was designed by what famous architect?
   A) Zaha Hadid B) Frank Gehry C) Le Corbusier

9. Gaining independence in 2011, what is the world's newest country?
   A) Kosovo B) South Sudan C) Montenegro

10. Hans Zimmer, the composer of the film soundtracks for *Gladiator* and the Dark Knight trilogy, is from which country?
    A) Germany B) Austria C) Australia

11. In which US city can you fly into Louis Armstrong airport?
    A) New Orleans B) Chicago C) St Louis

12. St Nicholas, from whom the modern day character of Santa Claus evolved, was born in which modern-day country?
A) Germany B) Finland C) Turkey

13. According to the UN, Europe is made up of how many countries?
A) 24 B) 44 C) 84

14. 'Once a jolly swagman camped by a billabong' is the opening line of what song, described as Australia's 'unofficial national anthem'?

15. These two volcanic mountains, known as Gros Piton and Petit Piton, stand on the coast of which Caribbean country?
A) Saint Lucia B) Dominica C) Grenada

16. The detective who solved *The Murder on the Orient Express* was from which country?
A) England B) France C) Belgium

17. The capital of the US state of Ohio is named after which explorer?

18. The Suez Canal connects the Mediterranean Sea with which body of water?

19. In the dry season, the main course of the Amazon River is normally no wider than 10km (6 miles). How wide can it get in the rainy season?
A) 30km (18 miles) B) 50km (30 miles) C) 80km (50 miles)

20. Ouagadougou is the capital of which African nation?
A) Burkina Faso B) Angola C) Zambia

Quiz 72 **Antarctica**

1. Though there are no permanent residents of Antarctica, how many people can usually be found living at its research stations in summer?
   A) 5000 B) 20,000 C) 10,000

2. In what year did the Norwegian explorer Roald Amundsen become the first person to reach the South Pole?
   A) 1888 B) 1911 C) 1924

3. The Antarctic Ice Sheet holds what percentage of the world's total surface fresh water?
   A) 50% B) 70% C) 90%

4. Antarctica is officially classed as a what?
   A) Island nation B) Desert C) National Park

5. What species of animal will you not find in the Antarctic?
   A) Polar bears B) Emperor penguins C) Killer whales

6. Although the rights and boundaries are much disputed, how many nations claim a portion of Antarctic territory as their own?
   A) Three B) Seven C) Fourteen

7. Which part of Antarctica is not claimed by any nation?
   A) Marie Byrd Land B) Ross Island C) Victoria Land

8. Of the seven continents, where does Antarctica rank in size order?
   A) Fifth B) Sixth C) Seventh

9. What is the average annual inland temperature in Antarctica?
   A) –7°C (–19°F) B) –37°C (1°F) C) –57°C (-71°F)

10. Which of these is not a genuine Antarctic island?
    A) Penguin Island
    B) Killer Whale Island
    C) Elephant Island

11. Ross Island is famed for which natural phenomena, not found on the mainland of the continent?
    A) Trees B) Hot springs C) Active volcanoes

12. Antarctica holds many records as a continent, but which of these is it not?
    A) The driest B) The lowest C) The windiest

13. McMurdo is the largest research station in Antarctica. To what country does it belong?
    A) USA B) Russia C) Chile

14. How many countries have scientists and researchers working at Antarctic research stations?
    A) 15 B) 30 C) 70

15. What is the name of the Southern Hemisphere's equivalent of the Aurora Borealis or Northern Lights?

16. What was Deception Island formerly used as?
    A) A nuclear waste dump B) A whaling station C) A prison

17. Roughly how many tourists visit Antarctica each year?
    A) 10,000 B) 60,000 C) 250,000

18. The largely barren Heard Island and the McDonald Islands are external Antarctic territories of which country?
    A) UK B) Australia C) New Zealand

19. In January 1978, Emilio Marcos Palma became the first human to do what in Antarctica?
    A) Be born
    B) Canoe around the entire continent
    C) Spend a year living as a penguin

20. Millions of years ago, Antarctica enjoyed a hot, tropical climate. True or false?

Quiz 73 **Dams Around the World**

1. Roughly what percentage of the world's total energy currently comes from dams?
   A) 6% B) 16% C) 60%

2. How much of the world's renewable energy comes from dams?
   A) 7% B) 35% C) 71%

3. Roughly how many dams are there across the world?
   A) 20,000 B) 60,000 C) 100,000

4. The remains of the world's oldest dam are in which country?
   A) Jordan B) Egypt C) China

5. The Three Gorges Dam, which has the largest hydroelectric capacity of any dam, lies on which Chinese river?

6. What is the name of the enormous dam on the Paraná river bordering Brazil and Paraguay?
   A) Tarbela Dam B) Aswan Dam C) Itaipu Dam

7. By area, Lake Volta is the world's largest dam reservoir. In what country would you find it?
   A) Venezuela B) Ghana C) Japan

8. The US Hoover Dam sits on which river?
   A) Colorado B) Mississippi C) St Lawrence

9. What is the name of its reservoir?
   A) Lake Tahoe B) Lake Mead C) Lake Okeechobee

10. Until 1947, the Hoover Dam was officially known as what?
    A) Rock Dam B) Boulder Dam C) Pebble Dam

11. The Contra Dam, also known as the Verzasca Dam, in Switzerland, features in the opening scene of which James Bond film?
    A) *Octopussy* B) *GoldenEye* C) *Die Another Day*

12. The Kariba Dam stands on the Zambezi River on the border between which two African countries?
    A) Morocco and Algeria
    B) Kenya and Tanzania
    C) Zambia and Zimbabwe

13. Monticello Dam, in California, USA, has a unique plughole-like spillway known as the Glory Hole that's become a popular unofficial venue for what sport?
    A) Skateboarding B) Soccer C) Street hockey

14. The Gordon Dam, the largest in Australia, is in which state?
    A) South Australia B) Victoria C) Tasmania

15. Which of these is not a genuine type of dam?
    A) Cantilever dam B) Buttress dam C) Arch dam

16. The world's biggest dam disaster occurred when the Banqiao Dam collapsed in 1976 in what country?
    A) USA B) India C) China

17. Added to many modern dams, what is a fish ladder?
    A) An access ladder, so called because the rungs are slippery
    B) A structure allowing fish to pass over and around a dam
    C) An opening through which workers can 'fish' for blockages

18. One of the world's tallest dams, the 300m (984ft) Nurek Dam is in which Central Asian country?
    A) Tajikistan B) Uzbekistan C) Kazakhstan

19. In an attempt to restore damaged ecosystems, how many dams have been removed from US waterways in the past century?
    A) Around 400 B) Around 1200 C) Around 1800

20. Created by the construction of the W.A.C. Bennet Dam in 1968, Williston Lake is a giant resevoir in which country?
    A) Canada B) USA C) UK

Quiz 74 **Russia**

1. The biggest country in the world, Russia takes up what percentage of the Earth's landmass?
   A) 1% B) 11% C) 21%

2. What is the national animal of Russia?
   A) The Siberian tiger B)The brown bear C) The golden eagle

3. How many time zones does Russia span?
   A) Five B) Seven C) Eleven

4. How many cities does the Trans-Siberian Railway, the world's longest train route, pass through?
   A) 57 B) 87 C) 117

5. In year was the Russian Revolution that overthrew the imperial family and led to the creation of the Soviet Union?

6. Who was the last Tsar of Russia?
   A) Alexander II B) Nicholas II C) Ivan III

7. What was the name of the Russian imperial family?
   A) Romanov B) Hapsburg C) Saxe-Coburg

8. During the last decades of their reign, the imperial family commissioned a series of elaborate jewelled eggs every Easter from which master jewellery firm?
   A) Tiffany B) Fabergé C) Cartier

9. With the most famous example sitting in the centre of Moscow, what is a Kremlin?
   A) A citadel B) A parliament building C) A country estate

10. What is the name of the multicoloured cathedral that stands next to Moscow's Kremlin?

11. In what century did Moscow suffer a devastating fire?
    A) 16th B) 18th C) 19th

12. The embalmed body of which Soviet leader is on display in a mausoleum in Moscow?

13. Which of these is not a genuine Moscow football team?
    A) FC Dynamo B) FC Spartak C) FC Sputnik

14. At what age did the founder of St Petersburg, Peter the Great become Tsar?
    A) Two B) Ten C) Twenty-one

15. Which of these is not a former name of St Petersburg?
    A) Petrograd B) Leningrad C) Volgograd

16. St Petersburg's White Nights Festival, held in June each year, celebrates what?
    A) The anniversary of the Russian National Ballet
    B) The long summer nights and the Midnight Sun
    C) The final melting of the winter snow

17. Soviet dictator Joseph Stalin wasn't born in Russia, but in which modern-day country?
    A) Georgia B) Ukraine C) Belarus

18. Located inside the Arctic Circle, what is the most northerly city (with a population of at least 100,000) in the world?
    A) Murmansk B) Norilsk C) Wrocław

19. In Moscow there's a statue dedicated to a dog who in 1957 became the first animal to orbit the Earth. What was her name?

20. What was the name of the spacecraft in which the Russian Yuri Gagarin became the first person to go into Space in 1961?
    A) *Vostok 1* B) *Soyuz 1* C) *Mir 1*

Quiz 75 Rivers and Lakes

1. What is the world's deepest river?
    A) The Nile B) The Congo C) The Amazon

2. By volume, what is the world's largest freshwater lake?
    A) Lake Baikal B) Lake Superior C) The Caspian Sea

3. The Nile is the longest, and the Amazon in the second longest,
    but what is the third longest river in the world?
    A) The Paraná B) The Yangtze C) The Lena

4. What percentage of the world's lakes are in Canada?
    A) 10% B) 30% C) 50%

5. What is the largest lake in Central America (Clue: it shares its
    name with one of the countries).

6. Which river splits the city of Budapest into its two sides,
    Buda and Pest?
    A) The Danube B) The Rhine C) The Elbe

7. The Uros people live on floating islands made of reeds in which
    high-altitude South American lake?

8. The Nile reaches the sea in Egypt, but in which country do its
    two main tributaries, the Blue Nile and the White Nile converge?
    A) Burundi B) Uganda C) Sudan

9. What is the largest lake in the UK?
    A) Lough Neagh, Northern Ireland
    B) Windermere, England
    C) Loch Lomond, Scotland

10. In what Southeast Asian country does the Mekong meet the sea?
    A) Laos B) Cambodia C) Vietnam

11. Malta has how many permanent lakes and rivers?
    A) 0 B) 10 C) Over 1000

12. Mesopotamia, the region where one of the world's first civilizations emerged, means 'between two rivers'. What rivers does it refer to?

13. Algae turn Australia's Lake Hillier what unusual colour?

14. The Mississippi River runs through ten US states. Which of these is not one of them?
   A) Tennessee B) Louisiana C) Georgia

15. Which of these is not the name of a genuine hot lake?
   A) Frying Pan Lake B) Boiling Lake C) Cappuccino Lake

16. These people are bathing in which river, sacred to followers of the Hindu faith?

17. Surrounding the picturesque Bled Island, in what European country would you find Lake Bled?
   A) Slovakia B) Slovenia C) Cyprus

18. There are five North American Great Lakes. Lake Superior is the largest (by surface area). What are the other four?
   You get a point for each.

19. What desert lake, which shrinks and grows with the seasons, contains Australia's lowest point, 15m (49ft) below sea level?
   A) Lake Eyre B) Lake Bumbunga C) Lake McKenzie

20. The Devil's Bath is a bright green, geothermal pool in what country?
   A) New Zealand B) Iceland C) Indonesia

Quiz 76 **General Travel Knowledge**

1. What continent has more countries than any other?

2. By what name is the ancient city of Byzantium now known?
   A) Istanbul B) Athens C) Jerusalem

3. Owing to its numerous overseas territories, which country spans the greatest number of time zones?
   A) UK B) USA C) France

4. Aside from the Sun at its centre, what two colours feature on the Argentinian flag?
   A) Blue and white B) Red and white C) Black and green

5. In what country has it become the tradition since the early 1970s to eat Kentucky Fried Chicken at Christmas?
   A) Brazil B) South Africa C) Japan

6. How many countries does the Equator pass through?
   A) 8 B) 13 C) 25

7. Which of these Italian cities is the furthest north?
   A) Milan B) Venice C) Turin

8. The Gulf Stream is a warm current that travels across which ocean?

9. What is the capital of Sudan?

10. What is the smallest of the seven 'stan' countries of Central Asia?
    A) Tajikistan B) Kazakhstan C) Turkmenistan

11. What does the name of the Serbian capital, Belgrade, mean?
    A) White City B) Beautiful City C) Big Hill

12. Having served in the British army for the past 200 years, the Gurkhas are soldiers who hail mainly from which country?
    A) Kenya B) Nepal C) Argentina

13. In the early 1500s, the Spanish conquistador Juan Ponce de León went searching in Florida, USA, for what?
A) The sunken city of Atlantis
B) The seven cities of gold known as Cibola
C) The Fountain of Youth

14. The three-day Tibetan festival of Losar celebrates what?
A) New Year B) Buddha's birthday C) The Dalai Lama's teachings

15. The Rogers and Hart song 'Manhattan', made famous by Ella Fitzgerald, begins with the line 'We'll have Manhattan'. What are the next two New York boroughs mentioned?

16. This huge waterfall, known as Skógafoss, is located on which island country?
A) Japan B) Iceland C) Madagascar

17. Which European country has had ten kings called Charles?
A) Scotland B) France C) Denmark

18. What does *Bafana Bafana*, the nickname of the South African football team mean?
A) Brave Brave B) The Boys The Boys C) Goals Goals

19. What are the only two landlocked countries in South America? You get a point for each.

20. By population, what is the largest city in Pakistan?
A) Lahore B) Islamabad C) Karachi

Quiz 77 **Car Travel**

1. The motor car was invented in 1885 in which country?
    A) USA B) France C) Germany

2. With over 300 million of them on its streets, which country has the most cars?
    A) USA B) China C) Germany

3. What small European country has the largest number of cars per person?
    A) San Marino B) Monaco C) Andorra

4. With what colour is the Italian sports car company Ferrari particularly associated?
    A) Red B) Black C) Yellow

5. What was the worldwide best-selling car brand in 2021?
    A) Fiat B) Toyota C) Volkswagen

6. Tata Motors are an automobile manufacturer based in which country?
    A) Indonesia B) Thailand C) India

7. Made between 1908–27, and one of the most popular cars of all time, the Ford Model T was only available in which colour?
    A) Green B) Blue C) Black

8. Organised by the Parisian magazine *Le Petit Journal*, in which year did (what is generally regarded as) the world's first motor race take place, between Paris and Bordeaux?
    A) 1894 B) 1900 C) 1912

9. What does Volkswagen mean?
    A) Electric vehicle B) The people's car C) Family wagon

10. In which country was the world's first purpose-built racetrack opened in 1907?

11. What animal appears on the Lamborghini logo?
    A) A snake B) A bull C) A horse

12. Which of these is not a Japanese car manufacturer? And, for a bonus point, in which country is this other manufacturer based?
    A) Nissan B) Toyota C) Kia

13. What make of car does the fictional British spy James Bond usually drive?
    A) Aston Martin B) Bentley C) Porsche

14. What is the name of the entrepreneur who is the CEO and 'product architect' of the electric car company Tesla in 2003?

15. In 1896, the British motorist Walter Arnold received the first ever speeding ticket. How fast was he going?
    A) 13kph (8mph) B) 20kph (12mph) C) 30kph (18pmh)

16. The world's first electric traffic light was installed in 1914 in which US city?
    A) Boston B) Cleveland C) Miami

17. In what year did the first Formula 1 racing competition take place?
    A) 1940 B) 1950 C) 1960

18. The racing driver Juan Manuel Fangio dominated the first decade of Formula 1 racing, winning the World Championship five times. What country was he from?
    A) Argentina B) Mexico C) Spain

19. Which luxury British car maker is also a noted manufacturer of aircraft engines?

20. What is an Argentinian city, a Spanish city and a car?
    A) Córdoba B) Mendoza C) Sevilla

Quiz 78 **New Zealand**

1. What is the capital of New Zealand?

2. How many official languages are there in New Zealand?
   A) One B) Three C) Five

3. What does *Aotearoa*, the Māori name for New Zealand mean?
   A) The land of the long white cloud
   B) The land of snow and ice
   C) The land of the many sheep

4. New Zealand is made up of two main islands, North Island and South Island. Which is bigger?

5. In addition to its two main ones, New Zealand has around how many other smaller islands?
   A) 200 B) 600 C) 1000

6. What is the body of water that divides the North and South Islands?
   A) Cook Strait B) Aotearoa Passage C) South Pass

7. What is the mountain range that spans much of the South Island?
   A) Southern Andes B) Southern Alps C) Southern Rockies

8. What percentage of the population is of Māori heritage?
   A) 6% B) 16% C) 46%

9. What is New Zealand's tallest mountain?
   A) Aoraki/Mount Cook B) Mount Taranaki C) Mount Tasman

10. What is New Zealand's longest river?
    A) Whanganui B) Waikato C) Oreti River

11. Roughly how far away is New Zealand from Australia?
    A) 750km (450 mi) B) 1500km (900 mi) C) 3000km (1850 mi)

12. The city of Queenstown is renowned for its what?
    A) Wineries B) Adventure sports C) Hot pools

13. What is the name of New Zealand's incredibly rare ground-living parrot of which there are less than 200 remaining individuals?
A) Kea B) Kiwi C) Kakapo

14. What animal outnumbers humans in New Zealand by five to one?
A) Sheep B) Kiwis C) Penguins

15. Taika Waititi is an award-winning New Zealand what?
A) Artist B) Swimmer C) Filmmaker

16. Who did the All Blacks defeat in the final of the first Rugby Union World Cup in 1987?
A) France B) England C) Australia

17. In Māori tradition, what is a hongi?
A) A war dance B) A greeting C) A savoury dish

18. Nicknamed the 'City of Sails' owing to its many yachts, and home to the Sky Tower, the country's tallest building, what is this city?
A) Auckland B) Christchurch C) Wellington

19. The North Island town of Rotorua is famed for its what?
A) Geysers and mud pools
B) Lord of the Rings sets
C) Rugby schools

20. What is the name of the Māori method for cooking food using heated rocks in an underground oven?
A) Haka B) Hāngī C) Hapu

 Answers on p.257 - 161 - Score

Quiz 79 **Southwest Europe**

1. Which country has more UNESCO World Heritage Sites, Spain or Portugal?

2. What are the two main colours on the Portuguese flag?
   A) Green and red B) Green and black C) Red and blue

3. Spain takes up what percentage of the Iberian Peninsula?
   A) 55% B) 95% C) 85%

4. Founded in 1732, Livravria Bertrand is the oldest bookshop in the world. In what Portuguese city can you browse its shelves?
   A) Lisbon B) Porto C) Faro

5. What mountain range separates Spain from France?

6. Found adorning buildings across Portugal, what are azulejos?
   A) Decorative tiles B) Window shutters C) Flower boxes

7. Which Spanish city is particularly associated with the work of the architect Antoni Gaudí?

8. The Portuguese footballer Cristiano Ronaldo played for nine seasons for which Spanish football club?

9. What were Spain and Portugal's respective currencies before they both adopted the Euro in the early 21st century?
   You get a point for each

10. Which of these alcoholic drinks is not produced in Portugal?
    A) Vinho Verde B) Ginja C) Orujo

11. If you ordered *calamares* in a Spanish tapas restaurant, what would you be served?
    A) Prawns B) Squid C) Octopus

- Regions -

12. Portugal is the world's largest producer of which material?
A) Cork B) Lace C) Leather

13. Held every year in the city of Buñol in Spain, the world's biggest (and messiest) food fight involves participants throwing over 100 tonnes of what?
A) Oranges B) Olives C) Tomatoes

14. What was the name of the Portuguese explorer who, from 1497–99, became the first known person to sail from Europe all the way around Africa to India?
A) Bartolomeu Dias B) Vasco da Gama C) Ferdinand Magellan

15. According to the official figures, which country's population has the highest proportion of Roman Catholics, Spain or Portugal?

16. Portugal has two official languages. Portuguese is one. What is the other?
A) Mirandese B) Lisboan C) Lusitanian

17. Which of these is not an official language of Spain, recognised by at least one of its regions?
A) Alsatian B) Galician C) Basque

18. What is the official language of Andorra?
A) Spanish B) Catalan C) French

19. Spain's highest mountain is not located on the mainland but on one of its islands. Which one?
A) Tenerife B) Menorca C) Ibiza

20. At what age did Spanish sporting superstar Rafael Nadal win his first Grand Slam tennis tournament, the French Open in 2005?
A) 17 B) 19 C) 21

Quiz 80 **The World of Literature**

1. Which of these US cities does not feature in the Beat Generation
   classic *On the Road* by Jack Kerouac?
   A) New Orleans B) San Francisco C) Salt Lake City

2. What sort of creatures are the Moomins, as featured in Finnish
   writer Tove Jansson's beloved children's books?
   A) Hippos B) Trolls C) Ghosts

3. *South* is which explorer's retelling of their epically ill-fated
   1914–17 voyage to Antarctica?
   A) Ernest Shackleton B) Roald Amundsen C) Robert Falcon Scott

4. The award-winning Japanese writer Haruki Murakami is a keen
   practitioner of which sport, which he has written about in depth?
   A) Marathon running B) Rock-climbing C) Canoeing

5. The Booker-winning novelist Margaret Atwood is from
   which country?

6. The *House of the Spirit*s and *City of Beasts* are works by which
   South American author?
   A) Jorge Luis Borges B) Mario Vargas Llosa C) Isabel Allende

7. How many novels did Charles Dickens write?
   A) 5 B) 15 C) 25

8. Henri Charrière's controversial 1969 'memoir' *Papillon* tells of
   his incarceration in the notorious penal colony Devil's Island in
   which French overseas territory?
   A) French Guiana B) French Polynesia C) Réunion

9. The hero of several Middle Eastern folk tales, Sinbad the Sailor
   hails from which city?
   A) Cairo, Egypt B) Baghdad, Iraq C) Mecca, Saudi Arabia

10. In which country is Salman Rushdie's *Midnight's Children* set?

11. What is the name of Jean Rhys' postconial prequel to Charlotte Brontë's *Jane Eyre*, set largely in Jamaica?

12. In what year were both Virginia Woolf and James Joyce born?
    A) 1822 B) 1882 C) 1912

13. Which of these novels was not written by the Russian novelist, Leo Tolstoy?
    A) *War and Peace* B) *Anna Karenina* C) *Madame Bovary*

14. What is the name of Brazilian author Paulo Coelho's allegorical wish-fulfilment novel of 1988, set in Spain and Egypt?

15. Which American author was the first Black woman to win the Nobel Prize for Literature?
    A) Toni Morrison B) Maya Angelou C) Alice Walker

16. *Things Fall Apart*, the debut novel of Chinua Achebe, tells of the 19th century European colonisation of which African country?
    A) Ghana B) Nigeria C) Kenya

17. Which Australian author has won the Booker Prize twice, once for *Oscar and Lucinda* in 1988, and then again for the *True History of the Kelly Gang* in 2001?
    A) Richard Flanagan B) Clive James C) Peter Carey

18. V.S. Naipaul, the author of the 1971 Booker winner, *In a Free State*, is from which Caribbean country?
    A) Barbados B) Trinidad and Tobago C) Jamaica

19. The epic 1300-plus page novel *A Suitable Boy*, published in 1993, is by which Indian author?
    A) Vikram Seth B) Arundhati Roy C) Amitav Ghosh

20. Louisa May Alcott's coming-of-age novel *Little Women* is set during which conflict?
    A) The American Revolutionary War
    B) The American Civil War
    C) The First World War

Quiz 81 **Around the Ancient World**

1. Sumer was the site of one of the world's earliest civilizations where some of the first cities were constructed. Where was it?
    A) Mesopotamia B) Mesoamerica C) Indus Valley

2. The ancient sea-trading civilization of Phoenicia was located mainly in what modern Middle Eastern country ?
    A) Saudi Arabia B) Lebanon C) Turkey

3. One of the Phoenicians' most valuable trading goods was a rich purple dye made from what?
    A) Crushed beetles B) Boiled sea snails C) Beetroot

4. Between around 600–1000 CE, the Tiwanaku civilization flourished on the banks of which large South American lake?

5. In what year was the Roman Empire founded?
    A) 753 BCE B) 146 BCE C) 27 BCE

6. The pre-Columbian Native American city of Cahokia lies close to which US river?
    A) Mississippi B) St Lawrence C) Colorado

7. The homes of the Indus Civilization, which thrived from around 2600–1800 BCE, are believed to have had the first what?
    A) Radiators B) Toilets C) Wall clocks

8. Who were the military dictators that ruled Japan from the 12th century to the mid-19th century?
    A) Samurai B) Shogun C) Chrysanthemum Emperors

9. The original Maya word for chocolate *xocolatl* translates as what?
    A) Sweet goodness B) Bitter water C) Smooth beans

10. What is the name of the stone city constructed by the Shona people in Southern Africa, which was abandoned in the 15th century?
    A) Great Zimbabwe B) Kilwa Kisiwani C) Nok Caves

11. What was the boundary erected by the Romans in around 122 CE to mark the northern extent of the province of Britannia?

12. The ancient Olympic Games were held every four years for over 1000 years. True or false?

13. The Terracotta Army, constructed in the third century BCE to protect the first Chinese emperor in the afterlife, was made up of roughly how many clay soldiers?
A) 80 B) 800 C) 8000

14. The Olmec civilization of ancient Mexico is perhaps best known for its giant statues of what body part?
A) Hands B) Heads C) Feet

15. Dating back to the early history of the Māori people of New Zealand , what is a Pā?
A) A hilltop fortress B) A forest shrine C) A wooden carving

16. Angkor Wat in Cambodia was originally built as a what?
A) Hindu temple B) Buddhist temple C) Mosque

17. What city was the capital of the Eastern Roman Empire and its successor, the Byzantine Empire, from 330 CE to 1453
A) Athens B) Constantinople C) Ravenna

18. What other regional power was responsible for finally conquering the Byzantine Empire?
A) Ottoman Empire B) Mughal Empire C) Abbasid Caliphate

19. Which of these leaders began building up the largest contiguous empire the world has ever seen?
A) Alexander the Great B) Julius Caesar C) Genghis Khan

20. The Triple Alliance is another name for the empire of which Mesoamerican civilisation?
A) Maya B) Aztecs C) Toltecs

Quiz 82 **East Africa**

1. Which East African nation's territory is 99% ocean?
    A) The Seychelles B) Mauritius C) Madagascar

2. In Ethiopia, the official calendar has how many months?
    A) Eleven B) Twelve C) Thirteen

3. Which East African nation has the longest coastline of any
    African country?
    A) Kenya B) Somalia C) Madagascar

4. Which of these statements about Mount Kilimanjaro is true?
    A) It forms part of the Atlas Mountains range
    B) It is the world's tallest mountain that doesn't form part of a range
    C) It last erupted in 1932

5. Mauritius was once home to the dodo. In what century did
    humans drive this ground-living bird to extinction?
    A) 17th B) 18th C) 19th

6. The Comoros is the world's leading producer of ylang-ylang
    plants, the oil of which is widely used to make what?
    A) Automobile lubricant B) Plastics C) Perfume

7. Which East African capital city has a national park on its southern
    border where you can see lions, zebras and other safari superstars?
    A) Nairobi, Kenya B) Dodoma, Tanzania C) Kigali, Rwanda

8. What is the capital of Uganda?

9. Madagascar is responsible for 80% of the world's supply of
    which product?
    A) Manioc B) Saffron C) Vanilla

10. Kenya's thriving technology and business district has been
    nicknamed what?
    A) Silicon Safari B) Silicon Savannah C) Silicon Oasis

11. Which city is home to the continent's largest street market?
    A) Asmara, Eritrea B) Addis Ababa, Ethiopia C) Mogadishu, Somalia

12. What is the name of the gorge in Tanzania where numerous
    remains of ancient humans have been found?
    A) Olduvai B) Naibor C) Ngorongoro

13. Often encountered in Sudan's deserts, what is a *haboob*?
    A) A flash flood B) A sand dune C) A dust storm

14. The Kenyan flag has an image of what at its centre?
    A) A sickle and and a sword
    B) A shield and two crossed spears
    C) An elephant and a lion

15. What is the only country where lemurs can be seen in the wild?
    A) Madagascar B) Tanzania C) Uganda

16. Rwanda's Volcanoes National Park is home to one of the only
    surviving populations of which critically endangered primate?

17. Both Kenya and Ethiopia are renowned for their middle-distance
    and long-distance runners. But which of these countries has won
    the most number of medals on the track at the Olympics?

18. Roughly how many animals (mainly wildebeest, gazelles and zebra)
    take part in the yearly Great Migration across the vast savannas of
    Tanzania and Kenya?
    A) 200,000 B) 2 million C) 20 million

19. What name was given to the fossilised skeleton of an
    Austalopithecus, a 3.2 million-year-old human ancestor
    disovered in 1974 in Ethiopia?
    A) Mary B) Lucy C) Raquel

20. *Ee Mungu Nguvu Yetu* is the national anthem of which East
    African nation?
    A) Kenya B) Ethiopia C) Tanzania

Quiz 83 **The World's Tallest Buildings**

1. At 146.6m (481ft), what was the tallest building in the world for over 3500 years from around 2570 BCE to the 13th century CE

2. From the 13th to the 19th century, all the world's tallest structures were what sort of building?
   A) Churches B) Castles C) Mosques

3. In 1884, the title of 'world's tallest structure' moved to the USA for the first time. What structure claimed it?

4. In 1889, France took top spot with the opening of the Eiffel Tower. How tall is it?
   A) 230m (755ft) B) 330m (1083ft) C) 430m (1411ft)

5. Which US building took over in 1930? It was the record holder for just 11 months until surpassed by the Empire State Building in 1931.

6. By contrast, the Empire State Building held the title until what year, when it was overtaken by New York's Twin Towers?
   A) 1960 B) 1970 C) 1980

7. What is the significance of the 1776ft (541m) height of One World Trade Center, the building that replaced the Twin Towers after it was destroyed in a terrorist attack in 2001?

8. The world's current tallest building, the 830m (2722ft) Burj Khalifa in Dubai UAE, opened in what year?
   A) 2005 B) 2010 C) 2015

9. What is the difference in temperature between the top and bottom of the Burj Khalifa?
   A) 2°C B) 7°C C) 15°C

10. What is the tallest building in a capital city?
    A) The Shard, London, UK
    B) The Lotte World Tower, Seoul, South Korea
    C) Tokyo Skytree, Tokyo, Japan

11. Which of these US cities has not at one time been home to the country's tallest skyscraper?
A) Philadelphia B) Chicago C) Las Vegas

12. Constructed in 1885, what building was considered the world's first ever skyscraper, despite being only 42m (138ft) tall?
A) The Singer Building, New York
B) The Home Insurance Building, Chicago
C) The Metropolitan Life Tower, New York

13. Africa's tallest building is a mosque, the Djamaa el Djazaïr, which has a 265m (869ft) high minaret. In what country would you find it?
A) Algeria B) Egypt C) Somalia

14. In what country is the tallest building in Europe?
A) Russia B) UK C) Spain

15. In what country is the tallest building in South America?
A) Brazil B) Argentina C) Chile

16. In what country is the tallest structure in the Southern Hemisphere?
A) Australia B) New Zealand C) South Africa

17. For many years, the world's tallest structure of any kind wasn't a skyscraper but a what, located in Warsaw, Poland?
A) Advertising hoarding B) Radio mast C) Flag pole

18. The Texaco Petronius oil platform is the world's tallest sea-based structure. How high does it stand above sea level?
A) 375m (1230ft) B) 427m (1400ft) C) 610m (2001ft)

19. What architectural feature do the Abraj Al Bait Towers in Mecca, the NTT Docomo Yoyogi Building in Tokyo, and the Palace of Culture and Science in Warsaw have in common?
A) Clock faces B) Spires C) Metal facades

20. Many skyscraper elevators travel at super speeds. How fast can the fastest travel?
A) 50kph (30mph) B) 75kph (45mph) C) 100kph (60mph)

Quiz 84 **Beijing**

1. Roughly, what is the population of Beijing?
   A) 6 million B) 11 million C) 21 million

2. That makes Beijing the largest city in China. True or false?

3. What is housed inside the Chairman Mao Memorial Hall?
   A) A gold statue of the former Chinese leader
   B) A mausoleum containing Mao's embalmed body
   C) A giant copy of Mao's Little Red Book

4. In what year were the Tiananmen Square student-led protests which were brutally put down by the governemnt?
   A) 1979 B) 1989 C) 1999

5. Hutongs are a feature of several cities of northern China. What are they?
   A) Traditional tea houses
   B) Homes with central courtyards
   C) Narrow lanes

6. The home of Chinese imperial power until the early 1900s, in what century was the Forbidden City built?
   A) 10th B) 15th C) 17th

7. How many rooms are there in the giant Forbidden City complex?
   A) 250 B) 4000 C) 9000

8. What official colour is the Forbidden City?
   A) Red B) Purple C) Green

9. What form of exercise can be seen being practised in parks and green spaces across Beijing?
   A) Tai chi B) Judo C) Table tennis

10. How many UNESCO World Heritage Sites are there in Beijing?
    A) Two B) Four C) Seven

11. Beijing has changed its name numerous times throughout its history. Which of these is not a former name of the city?
A) Jicheng B) Nanjing C) Zhongdu

12. Beijing used to be known as Beiping. True or false?

13. The city has a history stretching back over 3000 years, but in what century was it first made China's capital?
A) 2nd century BCE B) 13th century CE C) 20th century

14. In what year did Beijing host the Summer Olympic Games?
A) 1948 B) 1988 C) 2008

15. The stadium built to host the athletics events, and which has subsequently become the national stadium, was given what nickname, owing to its distinctive appearance?
A) The Fish Tank B) The Bird's Nest C) The Volcano

16. Which of these statements about Beijing is true?
A) It is the only city to have hosted both Summer and Winter Olympic Games
B) It has more skyscrapers than any other city
C) It is home to the world's largest street food market

17. What is the main language spoken in Beijing?
A) Mandarin B) Cantonese C) Hunanese

18. Which of these is a major thoroughfare in Beijing, running east to west across the city?
A) The Bund B) Chang'an Avenue C) Ye Woo Street

19. What famed dish is known locally as *kaoya*?
A) Roast duck B) Sweet and sour pork C) Ma-po tofu

20. How many international airports are there serving Beijing?
A) One B) Two C) Three

Quiz 85 **Roads and Routes**

1. The world's longest possible overland walking route, requiring no flights or boat crossings, stretches for 22,000km (14,000 miles) from Cape Town, South Africa, to where?
    A) Magadan, Russia B) Hanoi, Vietnam C) Mehamn, Norway

2. The *Canterbury Tales*, Geoffrey Chaucer's account of 31 pilgrims on their way from London to Canterbury, was written in what century?
    A) 13th B) 14th C) 15th

3. What is the famous former US highway, immortalised in various books and songs, that ran between Chicago and Santa Monica?

4. The Lycian Way is a long-distance hiking trail stretching for over 500km through which Mediterranean country?
    A) Greece B) Cyprus C) Turkey

5. What is the pilgrimage to the holy city of Mecca that all financially and physically able Muslims must make at least once in their life?

6. Why were the roads of ancient Rome straight?
    A) Because it made them cheaper to build
    B) Because Roman technology only allowed for straight roads
    C) Because it let Roman soldiers move as quickly as possible

7. Linking Pakistan with China, which 1300km (800 mile) mountainous highway, one of the highest paved roads in the world, was once part of the ancient Silk Road trading route?
    A) Pamir Highway B) Karakoram Highway C) San Bernardino Pass

8. What is the name of the highest point on the Inca Trail, the road leading to the mountaintop citadel of Macchu Picchu?
    A) Dead Woman's Pass B) Pizarro Pass C) The Andean Drop

9. In what country can you drive the Wild Atlantic Way, the longest uninterrupted coastal route in the world at 2500km (1553 miles)?
    A) Ireland B) South Africa C) Canada

10. Traditionally (if not entirely accurately), what are the two furthest points on mainland Britain, set 1407km (874 miles) apart?

11. Walkers of the Camino de Santiago, a popular medieval pilgrimage route through several European countries to Santiago de Compostela in Galicia, Spain, can help find their way by looking out for symbols showing what?
    A) A fish B) A scallop shell C) Loaves of bread

12. What famous Italian coast does the Strada Statale 163 follow?
    A) The Amalfi Coast B) The Ligurian Coast C) The Sicilian Coast

13. Now mainly used a cycle route since a new highway was opened in 2006, the North Yungas Road, once named the 'world's most dangerous road' is in which country?
    A) Russia B) Peru C) New Zealand

14. In what year did the world's first motor roadtrip take place?
    A) 1888 B) 1908 C) 1928

15. In which American city can you find the extremely steep and windy Lombard Street, known as 'the crookedest street in the world'?
    A) New York B) Phoenix C) San Francisco

16. In which South American country can you undertake the W Trek?

17. The GR20 is a footpath across which Mediterranean island?
    A) Malta B) Corfu C) Corsica

18. In what country could you hike the Tongariro Alpine Crossing?
    A) Austria B) Italy C) New Zealand

19. Which 240km (150-mile) Australian road was built by dug soldiers who had returned from the First World War?
    A) The Big Lap B) The Great Ocean Road C) Gibb River Road

20. The Kumano Kodo is an ancient pilgrimage trail in which country?
    A) Japan B) Indonesia C) India

Quiz 86 **General Travel Knowledge**

1. What is the Pacific Ocean's smallest country?
   A) Palau B) Tuvalu C) Nauru

2. The Lantern Festival marks the first day of Chinese New Year.
   True of false?

3. Which country has the world's tallest population, on average?
   A) The Netherlands B) Argentina C) Nepal

4. With almost 50% of its population under the age of 15, what
   country has the world's youngest population?
   A) Niger B) Colombia C) Papua New Guinea

5. Fireflies, deep-sea angler fish and certain types of plankton can
   all naturally glow in the dark, a phenomenon known as what?

6. In which year did Nelson Mandela become president of
   South Africa?
   A) 1982 B) 1994 C) 1999

7. What is the capital of the US state of California?
   A) Los Angeles B) San Diego C) Sacramento

8. In which of these chilly places would you find the musk ox,
   which has a thick, shaggy coat to protect it against the cold?
   A) The Arctic B) The Himalayas C) The Andes

9. What is the ceremonial Māori warrior dance famously performed
   by the All Blacks rugby team before their matches?
   A) The Hopak B) The Haka C) The Zaouli

10. The festival of Junkanoo is held in the countries of which region?
    A) Polynesia B) The Caribbean C) Southeast Asia

11. The Amazon River used to flow into the Pacific. True or false?

12. Gardens by the Bay is a waterfront nature park in which Asian city?
    A) Shanghai, China B) Singapore City C) Mumbai, India

13. What is the correct name for the species of whale commonly seen off the coasts of South Africa and Argentina
    A) Southern-right whale
    B) Eastern grey whale
    C) Northern sperm whale

14. Which country has the highest percentage of its land mass covered in forest?
    A) Suriname B) Finland C) Canada

15. Rarebit, a dish made of cheese (often mixed with ale and mustard) on toast is particularly associated with which British country?
    A) Scotland B) England C) Wales

16. What is the most commonly spoken language in the US after English?

17. Kaeng Massaman and Tom Yum Goong are dishes from the cuisine of which country?
    A) India B) Thailand C) Vietnam

18. What is the largest island off the west coast of North America?

19. What country has the world's largest sports stadium, by capacity?
    A) Brazil B) North Korea C) India

20. Which shopping centre in Midtown Manhattan, New York, is famous for its annual Christmas tree?
    A) Manhattan Mall
    B) The Rockefeller Center
    C) The Fulton Center

Quiz 87 **National Parks**

1. Established in the USA, which of these was the world's first national park?
    A) Yellowstone B) Yosemite C) Rocky Mountain

2. And in what year was it founded?
    A) 1822 B) 1872 C) 1922

3. Today, how many national parks are there in the USA?
    A) 23 B) 63 C) 633

4. Which state is home the largest number of national parks?
    A) Oregon B) California C) Nevada

5. What country has the world's highest number of national parks?
    A) USA B) South Africa C) Australia

6. What is the world's largest national park?
    A) Fiordland National Park, New Zealand
    B) Northeast Greenland National Park, Greenland
    C) Yugyd Va National Park, Russia

7. Bandhavgarh National Park in India is home to the world's largest concentration of what animal?
    A) Asian elephants B) Bengal tigers C) Reticulated pythons

8. What British national park makes up over 2% of the total area of Great Britain?
    A) Lake District, England
    B) Brecon Beacons, Wales
    C) Cairngorms, Scotland

9. What is Venezuela's Canaima National Park home to what?
    A) The world's deepest rainforest
    B) The world's highest waterfall
    C) World's highest flat-topped mountain

10. The Grand Canyon is in Great Basin National Park? True or false?

11. Tortuguero National Park in Costa Rica is named after what animal, its most famous annual visitors?
    A) Tapirs B) Turtles C) Toucans

12. In which European national park region can you see polar bears?
    A) Nordvest-Spitsbergen National Park, Norway
    B) Elk Island, Russia
    C) Sarek National Park, Sweden

13. One of the largest protected areas in Africa, in what country would you find the Selous Game Reserve?
    A) South Africa B) Tanzania C) The Gambia

14. What is the name of Slovenia's only national park, named after the country's highest mountain, located in the Julian Alps?
    A) Triglav B) Ljubljana C) Durmitor

15. Every year in the dry season, hundreds of elephants congregate at the reservoir in Sri Lanka's Minneriya National Park. By what name is this event known?
    A) The Gathering B) The Trumpeting C) The Pride of Sri Lanka

16. In what country's national parks can you see the world's largest concentration of wild lions?
    A) Tanzania B) Botswana C) South Africa

17. In which US state can you find the swampy wetlands of the Everglades National Park?
    A) Florida B) California C) Hawaii

18. In what Asian country would you find Khao Sok National Park?
    A) Thailand B) Laos C) Cambodia

19. Bindarri, Gundabooka and Murramarang are all national parks in which country?
    A) New Zealand B) Canada C) Australia

20. In what year did the first World Parks Congress take place?
    A) 1962 B) 1972 C) 1982

Quiz 88 **Brazil**

1. By area, Brazil is the what largest country in the world?
   A) Second B) Fifth C) Seventh

2. How many countries have land borders with Brazil?
   A) Three B) Six C) Nine

3. In what year did Brazil achieve independence?
   A) 1822 B) 1872 C) 1922

4. Brazil is named after what?
   A) A type of tree B) An indigenous song C) A rainforest tribe

5. What is Brazil's currency?
   A) The Brazilian peso B) The Brazilian real C) The Brazilian dollar

6. Aside from the capital, Brasília, which forms a separate federal district, how many states are there in Brazil?
   A) 12 B) 26 C) 55

7. Brazil's favelas or shanty towns take their name from what?
   A) A type of tree B) An indigenous song C) A rainforest tribe

8. With a population of over 12 million people, what Brazilian city is the largest in the entire Southern Hemisphere?

9. Brazil has won the FIFA Men's World Cup five times. For 10 points, in what years did it win, and who were their opponents in each final?

10. Rio de Janeiro is the only South American city to have hosted the Olympic Games? True or false?

11. Which of these musical genres did not originate in Brazil?
    A) Axé B) Choro C) Merengue

12. The Amazon rainforest takes up how much of Brazil's land mass?
    A) 15% B) 40% C) 60%

13. Brazil is home to the largest population of people from which Asian county outside of that country's own borders?
A) Vietnam B) Japan C) China

14. Brazil doesn't have an official language. True or false?

15. When viewed from the air, what shape is the capital city, Brasília?
A) An airplane B) A crucifix C) A star

16. Which common type of fruit are all genetic clones from a mutation found on a tree in a Brazilian monastery in 1820?
A) Granny Smith apples B) Navel oranges C) Cantaloupe melons

17. What is a caipirinha?
A) A cocktail B) A traditional dance C) A hat

18. What is Capoeira?
A) Brazil's parliament B) A martial art C) Brazil's original name

19. The costumes, floats and musicians of the Rio Carnival are organised by Samba what?
A) Clubs B) Committees C) Schools

20. Found in Brazil's Amazon rainforest, what sort of bird is this?
A) A hornbill B) A toucan C) A macaw

Quiz 89 **The Middle East**

1. What is the most commonly spoken language in the Middle East?

2. If Egypt isn't considered part of the Middle East, what is the largest city in the Middle East, by population?
   A) Istanbul, Turkey B) Tehran, Iran C) Riyadh, Saudi Arabia

3. What is the only island nation in the Middle East?
   A) Bahrain B) Qatar C) Oman

4. Which Middle Eastern city has an artificial island shaped like a palm tree?
   A) Abu Dhabi B) Kuwait City C) Dubai

5. What is the main ingredient of the popular Middle Eastern dish, hummus?
   A) Lentils B) Courgettes C) Chickpeas

6. Found across the Middle East, and particularly associated with Turkey, what is a hammam?
   A) A public bath B) A woven carpet C) A mountain plateau

7. How many United Arab Emirates are there?
   A) Three B) Five C) Seven

8. And what is the UAE's capital?

9. Medina, the second holiest city in Islam, where the prophet Muhammad is buried, is in which country?
   A) Yemen B) Saudi Arabia C) Jerusalem

10. Which of these is not a traditional Turkish dish?
    A) Shish kebab B) Köfte C) Biryani

11. The flags of Turkey and Bahrain use the same colours on their flags. What are they?
    A) Red and white B) Red and green C) Black and white

12. Constructed by the ancient civilizations of Mesopotamia, what sort of structure was a ziggurat?
    A) A stepped temple tower
    B) A coastal lighthouse
    C) A desert water tower

13. The Treasury, the Monastery and the Palace Tomb are the popular names of sites in which ancient Middle Eastern city?
    A) Babylon, Iraq B) Petra, Jordan C) Damascus, Syria

14. The Sea of Galilee in Israel where, according to the Bible, Jesus walked on water, is the world's lowest salt-water lake. True or false?

15. In what country would you find the UNESCO World Heritage Site of Shibam Hadramawt? The town is famed for having the world's highest mud-brick buildings, from which it gets the nickname, 'The Manhattan of the Desert'?
    A) Jordan B) Yemen C) Lebanon

16. Perhaps the most famous landmarks in Kuwait, what are the Kuwait Towers ?
    A) A network of over 30 water storage towers
    B) A group of enormous desert rocks
    C) A pair of futuristic skyscrapers housing government offices

17. What is the square black building, the holiest site in Islam, that lies at the centre of the Masjid al-Haram mosque in Saudi Arabia?

18. Pamukkale is a famous thermal spring in Turkey where limestone deposits have created enormous banks of snow white terraces. What does Pamukkale mean in Turkish?
    A) White Hill B) Cotton Castle C) Sheep Spring

19. Across the world, every pet hamster is descended from a pair of animals caught in Syria in the 1930s. True or false?

20. By area, which is larger, Turkey or Saudi Arabia?

Quiz 90 **US Silhouette States**

Can you identify which US states these silhouettes represent from the three available options?

1.

A) New Jersey B) Alaska C) Kansas

2.

A) Iowa B) Alabama C) Nevada

3.

A) Colorado B) Arkansas C) Ohio

4.

A) Indiana B) Arizona C) Hawaii

5.

A) Maine B) New York C) Michigan

6.

A) Oregon B) Idaho C) Washington

- Countries -

7.

A) California B) Vermont C) Illinois

8.

A) Delaware B) Iowa C) Rhode Island

9.

A) Texas B) Wisconsin C) Virginia

10.

A) Pennsylvania B) Florida C) Georgia

11.

A) Arizona B) Louisiana C) Montana

12.

A) New Hampshire B) Ohio C) Maine

13.

A) Nebraska B) Oklahoma C) Iowa

14.

A) West Virginia B) Kentucky C) Utah

15.

A) Tennessee
B) Massachusetts
C) South Dakota

Quiz 91 **General Travel Knowledge**

1. What is the world's most biodiverse country, home to around 10% of the world's known species?
   A) Indonesia B) Kenya C) Brazil

2. What is the name of the fictional world in the 2009 film *Avatar*, the highest grossing movie of all time?
   A) Zion B) Atlantis C) Pandora

3. In what year did the *Mayflower* carry the Pilgrims from England to America where they founded the Plymouth colony?
   A) 1520 B) 1620 C) 1720

4. Which country has the highest number of centenarians – people who are 100 years old or over?
   A) Japan B) France C) New Zealand

5. How many time zones are there in Africa?
   A) Four B) Six C) Eight

6. In which US city would you find the Gateway Arch, the world's tallest arch?
   A) Washington DC B) St Louis C) Las Vegas

7. Blackpink, Bigbang and Girls' Generation are pop bands from which country?
   A) Australia B) South Korea C) USA

8. In what country is the Strait of Magellan, a navigable channel though the southern tip of South America
   A) Chile B) Argentina C) Peru

9. The three points marking the limits of the Bermuda Triangle, the area of the Atlantic Ocean where several ships and planes are supposed to have mysteriously disappeared, are Bermuda itself, Miami in Florida and which Caribbean island?
   A) Jamaica B) Cuba C) Puerto Rico

10. What is the name given to the super-continent, containing all the other continents, that existed from around 335 to 200 million years ago?
    A) Gondwanaland B) Pangaea C) Pannotia

11. The Spanish Steps are a tourist attraction in which European city?

12. How many national flags feature the colour purple?
    A) None B) Two C) 23

13. Native to China, the world's largest amphibian is what sort of animal?
    A) A frog B) A toad C) A salamander

14. Which country has won the most number of medals at the Winter Olympic Games?
    A) Norway B) Canada C) Russia

15. Which of these is not a genuine airport?
    A) Eek Airport B) Useless Loop Airport C) Idiot Airport

16. Roughly how many stars are there on the Hollywood Walk of Fame in Los Angeles, USA?
    A) 1500 B) 2500 C) 5000

17. Which country has won the FIFA Men's World Cup the most number of times
    A) Germany B) Brazil C) Italy

18. And which country has won the FIFA Women's World Cup the most number of times?
    A) Germany B) Brazil C) USA

19. How high are the eruptions of Steamboat Geyser in Yellowstone Park, USA, the world's tallest active geyser?
    A) 30m (100ft) B) 60m (200ft) C) 90m (300ft)

20. What is the capital of the Australian state of Tasmania?

Quiz 92 **Southeast Europe**

1. Just six lines long, Greece has the shortest national anthem in the world. True or false?

2. Which of these cities is not in Croatia?
    A) Dubrovnik B) Sarajevo C) Split

3. What was Greece's currency before it adopted the euro?

4. King Zog I was ruler of which country from 1928 until it was invaded by Italy in 1939?

5. Who was the Greek goddess of Victory?
    A) Athena B) Hera C) Nike

6. Who was the Roman version of the Greek god of the sea and storms, Poseidon?

7. Malta is made up of three main islands: Malta, Comino and what other island?

8. The Minoan civilisation, the precursor to the classical Greek civilisation that would later emerge on the mainland, lasted from around 2000–1000 BCE on which island?
    A) Corfu B) Crete C) Mykonos

9. In 2019, the country of Macedonia officially changed its name to what?

10. Which of these statements about the ancient Greek Olympics is false?
    A) All the athletes were male and competed in the nude
    B) Events included running, throwing, wrestling and swimming
    C) The champion boxer Melankomas never threw a punch

11. How many now independent countries once made up the nation of Yugoslavia?

12. Many examples of ancient Greek pottery have survived to
    the modern day. Some show red figures on a black background
    while others have black figures on a red background.
    What style came first?

13. What is the capital of Cyprus?

14. Famed for its windmills, and blue and white buildings, what
    Greek island is this?

15. The Maltese flag is red and white, and also features what symbol?
    A) A cross B) A castle C) An eye

16. Which of these Greek philosophers was born first?
    A) Socrates B) Plato C) Aristotle

17. The multiple Grand-Slam-winning tennis player Novak Djokovic
    is from which country?
    A) Montenegro B) Croatia C) Serbia

18. Greece's Mount Athos has 20 of which sort of establishment?
    A) Hotels B) Monasteries C) Discos

19. The neck tie was invented in which Southeast European country
    in the 17th century?
    A) Croatia B) Greece C) Bosnia and Herzegovina

20. Naxos is the largest of which Greek island group?
    A) The Dodecanese B) The Cyclades C) The Ionians

Quiz 93 **Mountains**

1. The 188 tallest mountains on Earth are all in Asia. True or false?

2. What is the name of the Hawaiian mountain which is the world's tallest if measured from the sea floor?
   A) Mauna Loa B) Mauna Kea C) Haleakalā

3. Olympus Mons, the tallest mountain in the Solar System, is how many times taller than Mount Everest?
   A) Twice B) Three times C) Ten times

4. Grand Mesa in Colorado, USA, is the world's largest what?
   A) Sandstone mountain B) Vertical cliff C) Flat-topped mountain

5. After Mount Kilimanjaro, what is Africa's second-tallest mountain?
   A) Mount Kenya B) Mount Toubkal C) Mount Cameroon

6. How tall is Mount Wycheproof in Australia, the world's smallest 'officially registered' mountain?
   A) 14.8m (19ft) B) 148m (486ft) C) 420m (1378ft)

7. Which of these is not a mountain in Europe?
   A) Damavand B) Grossglockner C) The Matterhorn

8. How many mountains are there higher than 8000m (26,200ft)?
   A) 4 B) 14 C) 28

9. The Karakoram mountain range extends through five Asian countries, Afghanistan, Tajikistan, Pakistan, and which other two?
   A) India and China
   B) Russia and Kazakhstan
   C) Ukraine and Turkey

10. How tall is Japan's tallest mountain, Mount Fuji?
    A) 2,776m (9108ft) B) 3,776m (12,388ft) C) 8,776m (28,793ft)

11. Which of these is not a Himalayan peak
    A) Mount Kosciuszko B) Annapurna C) Lhotse

12. What is the tallest mountain located on an island?
    A) Puncak Jaya, New Guinea
    B) Mount Etna, Sicily
    C) Mount Erebus, Ross Island

13. This is the picture of the base camp of which Himalayan mountain, visible in the distance?

14. Which of these mountain ranges is in Africa?
    A) Carpathians B) Virunga Mountains C) Western Ghats

15. Once known as Mount McKinley, what has been the name of North America's highest peak since 2015?

16. In what country would you find the Makhonjwa Mountains, believed to be the world's oldest with rocks dating back 3.6 billion years?
    A) China B) South Africa C) Australia

17. The Vinson Massif is the highest mountain where?
    A) The Arctic B) The Antarctic C) The Amazon

18. Growing at a rate of 7mm (0.3 inches) a year, it is believed that Nanga Parbat will overtake Everest as the world's highest peak in around 241,000 years. In what mountain range is it located?
    A) The Alps B) The Atlas Mountains C) The Himalayas

19. The peak closest to outer space isn't Mount Everest. True or false?

20. In what country is Ojos del Salado, the world's tallest volcano?
    A) Chile B) Brazil C) Spain

Quiz 94 **Germany**

1. In what year did Germany officially unify into a single country for the first time?
   A) 1483 B) 1871 C) 1918

2. And, following their division after the Second World War, when did West and East Germany reunify to form a single country again?
   A) 1980 B) 1990 C) 2000

3. Germany has Western Europe's largest population. True or false?

4. How many federal states are there in Germany?
   A) Eight B) Twelve C) Sixteen

5. Which city is Germany's economic hub and the home of the European Central Bank?

6. Who was German chancellor from 2005 to 2021?
   A) Helmut Kohl B) Gerhard Schröder C) Angela Merkel

7. Many of Berlin's major museums, including the Altes Museum and the Pergamonmuseum, are gathered where?
   A) On an island
   B) In a former royal palace
   C) In a disused airport

8. Roughly how many types of sausage are made in Germany?
   A) 800 B) 1200 C) 1600

9. Weisswurst is a white sausage traditionally served with which condiment?
   A) Sweet mustard B) Ketchup C) Mayonnaise

10. What is the capital and largest city in Bavaria?

11. By what name is the heavily wooded area of *Schwarzwald* in southwest Germany known in English?

12. Invented by Karl Drais in 1818, the *draisine*, or dandy horse, was an early version of which vehicle?
    A) The bicycle B) The motorcycle C) The motor car

13. Which German novelist wrote *Death in Venice*?

14. The German Beer Purity Law, or *Reinheitsgebot*, of 1516 states that beer can only be made from how many ingredients?
    A) Two B) Four C) Twenty

15. In what year was the Berlin Wall erected? And, for a bonus point, in what year was it torn down again?

16. What is this famous cathedral, seen here pictured next to the Hohenzollern Bridge?
    A) Aachen B) Cologne C) Mainz

17. Which of these composers is German?
    A) Frédéric Chopin B) Joseph Haydn C) Richard Wagner

18. In what century did Johannes Gutenberg invent the printing press?
    A) 13th B) 15th C) 17th

19. In 1920, during an attempted coup, which city temporarily became German's capital (the seat of the German government)?
    A) Stuttgart B) Hamburg C) Leipzig

20. No speed limit applies to more than 70% of Germany's motorway, or autobahn, network. True or false?

Quiz 95 **International Organisations**

1. The Treaty of Versailles formally ended the First World War and
   led to the creation of which international organisation?
   A) The League of Nations B) The United Nations C) FIFA

2. Despite playing a large role in its formation, which major combatant
   from the war didn't ultimately join this organisation?
   A) Germany B) France C) USA

3. Which international political and economic union can trace its
   roots back to the formation of the European Coal and Steel
   Community in 1951?
   A) UNESCO B) European Union C) NATO

4. The United Nations Environment Programme is headquartered
   in which African capital?
   A) Addis Ababa, Ethiopia B) Nairobi, Kenya C) Cairo, Egypt

5. Amnesty International is dedicated to the protection of what?
   A) Human rights B) The environment C) Free trade

6. OPEC is the inter-governmental organisation that controls the
   global oil market. What does OPEC stand for?

7. How many of the 13 members of OPEC can you name?
   You get a point for each?

8. The G7 is made up of the USA, the UK, Japan, Germany and
   what three other countries? You get a point for each.

9. Which animal is used as the logo of the World Widlife Fund?
   A) A black rhinoceros B) A mountain gorilla C) A panda

10. Which international humanitarian organisation was set up in
    1863 by the Swiss businessman Jean-Henri Dunant?
    A) UNICEF B) The Red Cross C) Doctors Without Borders

11. In what year was the military alliance NATO (North Atlantic Treaty Organization) established?
    A) 1939 B) 1949 C) 1959

12. What was the name of the rival Cold War treaty organisation made up of the USSR and Eastern Bloc states?

13. How many member states make up the European Union?
    A) 17 B) 27 C) 37

14. How many European countries have the Euro as their currency?
    A) 9 B) 19 C) 27

15. What European country is home to both the International Olympic Committee and FIFA, football's governing body?
    A) UK B) Switzerland C) Greece

16. What does UNESCO stand for?

17. Roughly, how many UNESCO World Heritage Sites are there?
    A) 100 B) 1100 C) 2100

18. In what city was the conference held in 1946 that led to the establishment of the United Nations?
    A) San Francisco, USA B) New York, USA C) Brussels, Belgium

19. Where are the headquarters of the United Nations?
    A) San Francisco, USA B) New York, USA C) Brussels, Belgium

20. The African Union, a group representing 55 countries in Africa, is headquartered where?
    A) Addis Ababa, Ethiopia
    B) Brussels, Belgium
    C) Kigali, Rwanda

Quiz 96 **General Travel Knowledge**

1. The island of Zanzibar forms part of which African country?
   A) Kenya B) Tanzania C) Madagascar

2. Japan is divided into 47 administrative districts known as what?
   A) States B) Prefectures C) Cantons

3. Which European capital city was built on 14 islands?
   A) Copenhagen B) Stockholm C) Rome

4. The Khao San Road is a busy, bustling street and a major tourist attraction in which Southeast Asian city?
   A) Phnom Penh, Cambodia
   B) Jakarta, Indonesia
   C) Bangkok, Thailand

5. Which major sea sits to the north of Turkey, to the east of Bulgaria and to the west of Georgia?
   A) Black Sea B) Caspian Sea C) Mediterranean Sea

6. What country gave the world the dish poutine, a combination of French fries, cheese and gravy?
   A) France B) Mali C) Canada

7. The Equator is framed by two major lines of latitude that lie 23.5° north and 23.5° south. What is the name of the southerly line?

8. Which country has the world's largest Muslim population?
   A) Saudi Arabia B) Indonesia C) Pakistan

9. In which year was Uluru, the original name for Ayers Rock in the language of the Pitjantjatjara Aboriginal people of central Australia, reintroduced?
   A) 1983 B) 1993 C) 2012

10. Every year, in the city of Lopburi in Thailand, a food festival is held in honour of which animal?
    A) Tiger B) Elephant C) Monkey

11. Located 54.8 degrees south of the Equator, Ushuaia is often claimed to be the southernmost city in the world. In what South American country would you find it?

12. In which US city can you visit the popular seafront neighbourhood known as Fisherman's Wharf?
A) San Francisco B) Seattle C) Miami

13. There's a hill on North Island, New Zealand, that is believed to have the world's longest place name. How many letters does it contain?
A) 25 B) 55 C) 85

14. Spain's northeast coast is known as the Costa Brava. What does Costa Brava mean?
A) Northern Coast B) Wild Coast C) Tranquil Coast

15. France's Michelin guides have been awarding stars for excellence to restaurants since 1904. What is the maximum number of stars an establishment can receive?
A) Three B) Five C) Ten

16. Which country was home to the first Legoland theme park?
A) USA B) Japan C) Denmark

17. In what year was the original Woodstock Music Festival held?
A) 1969 B) 1970 C) 1971

18. In which European country can you visit the historic walled city of Dubrovnik?
A) Czech Republic B) Croatia C) Cyprus

19. Pahoehoe, aa, blocky and pillow are the four main types of what natural phenomenon?
A) Wind B) Waves C) Lava

20. What Caribbean country is nicknamed the 'Spice Island'?
A) Cuba B) Grenada C) Saint Lucia

Quiz 97 **Canada**

1. What is the capital of Canada?
    A) Toronto B) Montreal C) Ottawa

2. By population, what is the largest city in Canada?
    A) Toronto B) Montreal C) Ottawa

3. Canada is divided into ten provinces and three territories.
    True or false?

4. By area, Canada is the what largest country in the world?
    A) Second B) Fifth C) Seventh

5. What is Canada's currency?
    A) Canadian dollar B) Canadian pound C) Canadian euro

6. What are the colours of the Canadian flag?

7. What is the national animal of Canada?
    A) Moose B) Beaver C) Grizzly bear

8. What is the largest animal in Canada?
    A) Moose B) Polar bear C) Wood bison

9. In what city would you find Canada's tallest structure, the
    553m (1815ft) CN Tower?
    A) Calgary B) Vancouver C) Toronto

10. What percentage of Canada's population lives within 250km
    (150 miles) of the country's southern border with the USA?
    A) 10% B) 50% C) 90%

11. What is Canada's largest island?
    A) Vancouver B) Baffin C) Newfoundland

12. Which of these is not one of Canada's national parks?
    A) Banff B) Jasper C) Denali

13. In winter, the Rideau Canal in Ontario becomes what?
    A) The world's largest Christmas market
    B) The world's largest skating rink
    C) The world's largest fairground

14. What is the name of the Canadian mountain that has the world's largest vertical drop, at 1675m (5495ft)?
    A) Mount Thor B) Mount Odin C) Mount Loki

15. Which Canadian company is the world's largest provider of circus-themed entertainment?

16. What is this a picture of?
    A) The Canadian Parliament Buildings
    B) Christ Church Cathedral, Vancouver
    C) The Royal Ontario Museum

17. Named after a famous explorer, what is the driving trail along the Cape Breton Highlands in Nova Scotia?
    A) The Cabot Trail B) The Columbus Trail C) The Erikson Trail

18. Numerous dinosaurs have been discovered in Alberta. Which of these is not a genuine Alberta dino?
    A) Albertosaurus B) Albertaceratops C) Albertaraptor

19. The Bay of Fundy has the world's highest what?
    A) Cliffs B) Tidal range C) Beaches

20. What is the name of the river in the Yukon Territory in the northwest where there was a major gold rush in the late 19th century?

Quiz 98 **The World of Art**

1. Which Italian Renaissance artist painted the ceiling of the Vatican City's Sistine Chapel?

2. Dedicated to Impressionist, Post-Impressionist and 20th-century art, in what city would you find the Artizon Museum?
   A) Tokyo, Japan B) New York, USA C) Athens, Greece

3. The Dutch artist Vincent van Gogh famously painted lots of sunflowers. But how many paintings make up his sunflower series?
   A) Three B) Six C) Twelve

4. Which of these products did the American pop artist Andy Warhol not feature in one of his multi-image works?
   A) Soup cans B) Coca Cola bottles C) Toothpaste tubes

5. Gongbi and Baimiao are painting techniques from which country's artistic tradition?
   A) India B) China C) Cambodia

6. What is the Italian term that emerged in the Renaissance to describe a strong contrast between light and shadow in an image?
   A) Chiaroscuro B) Grisaille C) Sgraffito

7. Famed for her black-and-white collages, often overlaid with captions, the artist Barbara Kruger is from what country?
   A) Austria B) Australia C) USA

8. What style of visual arts emerged out of the *Exposition Internationale des Arts Décoratifs et Industriels Modernes* in 1925?
   A) Cubism B) Art Deco C) Abstract Expressionism

9. Osamu Tezuka, Katsuhiro Otomo and Naoki Urasawa are (or were) leading protagonists in which Japanese art form?
   A) Calligraphy B) Manga C) Sculpture

10. In which Spanish city was the painter Pablo Picasso born?
    A) Málaga B) Bilbao C) Barcelona

11. The US painter Georgia O'Keeffe is particularly well known for her paintings of which US region?
    A) The Southwest B) Florida C) Alaska

12. In which city was Edvard Munch inspired to paint his most famous work, *The Scream*?
    A) Berlin, Germany B) Oslo, Norway C) Stockholm, Sweden

13. MALBA is a museum of Latin American art in which South American country?
    A) Colombia B) Brazil C) Argentina

14. Famously inventive, which of these contraptions did the Italian artist and polymath Leonardo da Vinci not come up with an idea for?
    A) The helicopter B) The jet engine C) The parachute

15. Famed for her paintings *Earth's Creation* and *Yam Dreaming*, Emily Kame Kngwarreye was an artist from which country?
    A) South Africa B) Papua New Guinea C) Australia

16. Which German architect founded the Bauhaus school of design in Weimar in 1919?
    A) Walter Gropius B) Max Ernst C) Otto Dix

17. Tassili n'Ajjer in Algeria, Laas Geel in Somalia and Lascaux in France are well known for what type of art?
    A) Cave paintings B) Rock sculptures C) Pop-art murals

18. The Japanese artist Hokusai is perhaps best known for his print T*he Great Wave off Kanagawa* which features in a series of 36 views of which iconic landmark?
    A) Mount Fuji B) Himeji Castle C) Fushimi Inari-Taisha

19. Which North American artist taught herself to paint while recovering from a bus accident?
    A) Frida Kahlo B) Mary Cassatt C) Mickalene Thomas

20. The Renaissance painter Titian was from which Italian city?
    A) Venice B) Rome C) Florence

 Score

Quiz 99 **The Arctic**

1. How many countries have territory within the Arctic Circle?
   A) Four B) Six C) Eight

2. Roughly how many people live above the Arctic Circle?
   A) 400,000 B) 4 million C) 40 million

3. The Arctic Circle lies at approximately what latitude north?
   A) 45° B) 66° C) 90°

4. The word 'Arctic' is derived from the Greek word for what?
   A) Snow B) Bear C) North

5. In what year did the explorers Robert Peary and Matthew Henson claim to have become the first people to set foot on the North Pole?
   A) 1899 B) 1909 C) 1929

6. What is the popular name for the phenomenon by which the Sun doesn't fully sink below the horizon in the Arctic in summer for over 70 days?

7. Why did an Arctic iceberg make headlines all over the world in 1912?

8. How many species of animal can be found living in the Arctic?
   A) 2500 B) 5500 C) 10,500

9. What animal is on the logo of the Arctic Council, the inter-governmental body representing Arctic countries?
   A) Polar bear B) Walrus C) Arctic fox

10. The Arctic spans how many time zones?
    A) None B) One C) Twenty-four

11. Roughly what percentage of Greenland is covered in ice?
    A) 40% B) 60% C) 80%

12. The Viking who established the first European settlement on Greenland (and gave it its name) was Erik the what?
A) Red B) Green C) Relentless

13. The Arctic Ocean is the smallest and coldest ocean. True or false?

14. The town of Churchill in the province of Manitoba, south of the Arctic Circle, is famous for being one of the best places in the world to spot which animal?
A) Polar bears B) Humpback whales C) Reindeer

15. Unlike the South Pole, which sits on land, the North Pole is located on (almost) permanently frozen ocean? True or false?

16. Two of these seals live in the Antarctic, while one lives in the Arctic. Which one?
A) Harp seal B) Weddell seal C) Leopard seal

17. The Greenland shark, found in the waters of the Arctic Ocean, holds what claim to fame?
A) It's the world's deepest living fish
B) It has the longest lifespan of any vertebrate
C) It's the world's largest shark

18. What is the name for the top layer of soil in the Arctic that never thaws?
A) Permafrost B) Tundra C) Chaparral

19. Arctic ice makes up what percentage of the Earth's freshwater?
A) 1% B) 10% C) 50%

20. What is the name of the sailing route across the top of North America through the Arctic Ocean sought by sailors since the 15th century but which, owing to frozen seas and hazardous conditions, was only finally navigated in the early 20th century?

Quiz 100 **Borders Around the World**

1. Mont Blanc, Western Europe's highest mountain, lies on the border of which two countries?
   A) France, Switzerland B) France, Italy C) Switzerland, Austria

2. China and Russia share the record for the most international land borders. How many is that?
   A) 9 B) 14 C) 21

3. Boundary Lake is a small lake that lies on the border of which two countries?

4. The USA shares land borders with how many countries?
   A) Two B) Three C) Four

5. The Large Hadron Collider, the world's largest particle accelerator, lies deep underground on the border between which two European countries?

6. When the Rio Grande crosses the border from the USA to Mexico, its name changes to what?

7. Offa's Dyke is an eighth-century linear earthwork marking the border between which two Western European countries?

8. What is the only South American country with a border on both the Atlantic and Pacific Oceans?

9. Niagara Falls lies on the border of which two countries?

10. Which African country has the largest number of land borders?
    A) Uganda B) Democratic Republic of Congo C) Mali

11. Afghanistan is bordered by Pakistan, Turkmenistan, Uzbekistan, Tajikistan, China and which other country to the southwest?

12. Victoria Falls lies on the border of which two African countries?

13. What tiny country has the world's shortest coastline?

14. As a proportion of its entire land border, what country has the shortest coastline in the world
    A) Bolivia B) Bosnia and Herzegovina C) Thailand

15. An enclave country, Lesotho is entirely surrounded by what other African country?

16. What's the minimum number of borders you need to travel through to get from Finland to North Korea?

17. Which river forms part of the boundary between Laos and Thailand?
    A) Yangtze B) Mekong C) Salween

18. What is the name of the area within Europe where no border controls apply, allowing citizens of member states to travel freely between countries?

19. Papua New Guinea has a western land border with which country?
    A) Indonesia B) Malaysia C) Australia

20. New South Wales shares borders with all the other mainland Australian states. True or false?

21. What two countries border Andorra in Western Europe?

22. Croatia shares a land border with Italy. True or false?

23. What two countries border Vietnam to the west?

24. Which of these countries does not share a border with Egypt?
    A) Libya B) Sudan C) Saudi Arabia

25. Which of these countries does not share a border with Argentina?
    A) Peru B) Chile C) Bolivia

Answers

Quiz 1 **Around the World in 25 Countries**

1. Canada

2. A) Ecuador

3. C) Ethiopia

4. B) Jamaica

5. C) Pakistan

6. A) Australia. It's a sponge cake covered in chocolate icing and desiccated coconut.

7. B) China

8. Denmark and Sweden

9. C) Peru. It's built near a high-altitude gold mine.

10. New Zealand

11. B) Tanzania. You could also see the zebras in Kenya, but you'd be in the Masai Mara Game Reserve.

12. Brazil

13. C) USA

14. Papua New Guinea

15. France. It's French Guiana, the largest part of the European Union not on the European continent.

16. Libya

17. Scotland

18. Albania

19. A) Colombia

20. Indonesia

21. C) Russia. The coldest city of all is Yakutsk, which lies only 450km (280 miles) south of the Arctic Circle where average temperatures are −7.5°C (18.5°F) and a record low of −64.4°C (−83.9°F) has been recorded.

22. Vatican City. It's a tiny self-governing enclave within the city of Rome, Italy.

23. B) Somalia

24. Poland

25. C) Argentina

Quiz 2 **The World of Wildlife**

1. The skunk (the striped skunk, to be precise).

2. A) A jaguar from South America. It has a similar coat to a leopard's, except its rosettes have a spot in the middle, whereas leopard rosettes don't. Tigers, of course, are striped.

3. C) Goat

Answers

4. Bats.

5. True, they belong to the same family as polar bears and brown bears, but feed almost exclusively on bamboo plants.

6. A) Carpet sharks

7. Bison

8. C) Fish. It's the sunfish, the world's heaviest bony fish.

9. C) India. There's a small population of Asiatic lions in the country's Gir Forest.

10. B) South America

11. A) Purple

12. The Komodo dragon

13. C) A small marsupial from Australia

14. The killer whale, or orca

15. B) Rodent

16. C) Polar bear

17. South Africa

18. B) 22 months

19. A) Bird. It's the national bird of both El Salvador (where it's known as the Torogoz) and Nicaragua (where it's known as the Guardabarranco).

20. C) They spin their tails to scatter their poo as it comes out, in order to mark their territory.

Quiz 3 **North Africa**

1. C) 31%

2. A) Desert (in Arabic)

3. One

4. Rabat

5. Tunisia

6. Arabic

7. Algeria

8. Tagine. The stews cooked inside the dish are also known as tagines.

9. Tuareg

10. A) Fortress

11. B) 2011

12. B) 14km (9 miles)

13. Morocco and Spain

14. Sirocco

15. Tunisia

16. Fennec fox

Answers

17. B) Atlas Mountains

18. The Sahel

19. A) A large flat area of sand in a desert

20. Cairo in Egypt, with over 21 million people living in the greater metropolitan area.

Quiz 4 **Festivals Around the World**

1. Munich

2. B) Fat Tuesday

3. Marigolds

4. November (on 1st and 2nd day of the month)

5. Notting Hill

6. 26 January

7. C) Every two years (which is what Biennale means)

8. C) Kenya

9. B) Money in a red envelope

10. A) Fried food

11. Berlin

12. B) Sambadrome

13. Hanukkah

14. Japan

15. Paris, Milan, London and New York

16. Coachella (formally, the Coachella Valley Music and Arts Festival)

17. C) New Zealand (in Auckland)

18. 17 March

19. B) 1970

20. A) Crop Over

Quiz 5 **Airports**

1. Delhi. It's Indira Gandhi International Airport.

2. Paris

3. A) Sydney

4. C) Kingston, Jamaica

5. B) Atlanta. It's Hartsfield–Jackson Atlanta International Airport.

6. C) Croydon Airport, which prior to the Second World War was London's main commercial airport

7. B) It has a railway line that cuts across the runway.

8. Bangkok. It's Suvarnabhumi International Airport.

Answers

9. A) Beijing, China. It's the Beijing Daxing airport, which covers an area of over 696,773 sq m (7.5 million sq ft).

10. B) 175km (109 miles)

11. False. Travellers can visit a tropical butterfly garden.

12. A) It's the world's oldest continuously operated airport, having been established in 1909 as a location for Wilbur Wright (of first-powered flight, Wright Brothers fame) to train military pilots.

13. Johannesburg. It's O.R. Tambo International Airport.

14. B) Turkey

15. C) 8

16. A) China. It's at Beijing's Daxing International Airport.

17. Cristiano Ronaldo

18. C) Kenya. It's named after the country's former president.

19. C) Mozart

20. John F. Kennedy Airport (JFK). It was renamed in honour of the recently assassinated president.

Quiz 6 **USA**

1. The bald eagle

2. Hawaii. It became a state in August, 1959. Alaska had become the 49th state in January that same year. Puerto Rico isn't a state but an 'unincorporated territory' of the USA.

3. The Star Spangled Banner

4. The Potomac River

5. California, Oregon, Washington, Alaska and Hawaii

6. C) Aluminium, which at the time was one of the most expensive metals on Earth. However, a new extraction process was invented soon after and, as aluminium is the most abundant metal in Earth's crust, its value soon plummeted.

7. Richmond, Virginia

8. B) One World Trade Center at 541m (1776ft)

9. A) A stew

10. Three: Iowa, Ohio and Utah

11. A) Texas Rangers. The Dallas Mavericks are a basketball team and the Houston Texans are an American football team based in Houston.

12. Harriet Tubman

13. John Steinbeck

14. B) Theodore Roosevelt

Answers

15. The are 50 stars, representing the 50 states, and 13 stripes, representing the original 13 colonies.

16. B) Los Angeles

17. Mojave Desert

18. A) Poisonous lizard

19. Broadway

20. C) Rhode Island (Delaware is the second smallest and Connecticut is the third smallest)

Quiz 7 Rio de Janeiro

1. B) 16th century. On 1 March, 1565.

2. C) 2016

3. C) There isn't one. When the Portuguese explorer Gaspar de Lemos first arrived in the area in 1502, he mistook the giant bay here for a river, which he named after the month of his arrival, Janeiro ('January')

4. A) Maracanã. It hosted the largest ever football crowd when 199,854 people saw Brazil lose the 1950 World Cup Final to Uruguay.

5. C) Five, from the Friday to the Tuesday before Ash Wednesday.

6. A) Samba.

7. B) Sugar Loaf Mountain

8. True. Following Napoleon's invasion of Portugal, the royal family fled to Brazil where, from 1808–21, Rio de Janeiro acted as the capital of the Kingdom of Portugal

9. B) 1960, when it was moved to the newly built Brasilia

10. A) Cariocas

11. C) The stars. They represent the constellations that were above Rio on November 15, 1889, the day the country changed from an empire to a republic.

12 Bossa nova, which literally means 'new wave'.

13 B) 30m (98ft).

14. A) Corcovado

15. Copacabana

16. C) Guanabara Bay

17. C) The Museum of Tomorrow (*Museu do Amanhã*).

18. A) The Tupi

19. B) Coffee

20. C) 2012

Answers

Quiz 8 **Northern Europe**

1. The Vikings

2. Helsinki

3. Surtsey (named after a fire giant from Norse mythology)

4. The Northern Lights

5. C) Seeds. Svalbard is home to the Global Seed Vault, a giant biodiversity backup facility, where over a million seed species are stored.

6. A) Norway

7. Fjords

8. B) Lithuania

9. The Arctic tern

10. Amber (fossilized tree sap)

11. B) Finland

12. The Little Mermaid

13. A) Fermented fish (herring)

14. A) Mid-Atlantic Ridge

15. Sami

16. Denmark

17. B) Norwegian Sea

18. B) 930 CE

19. C) Oslo

20. A) An ice hotel

Quiz 9 **Wonders of the World**

1. The Hanging Gardens of Babylon. Supposedly built by King Nebuchadnezzar II (605–562 BCE) to replicate the homeland of his homesick Persian wife, the gardens remains have never been located.

2. A) Zeus

3. A) Statue

4. B) Ephesus in Turkey. Once one of the greatest temples of the ancient world, today the site is marked by a single column.

5. The Great Pyramid at Giza

6. C) Turkey

7. The Panama Canal

8. Brazil

9. The CN Tower in Toronto, Canada

10. B) 1994

11. The Netherlands

Answers

12. King Kong

13. The Colosseum in Rome

14. The Christ the Redeemer statue in Rio de Janeiro, Brazil

15. C) 15th century CE

16. C) 20th century. Although it had long been known about by locals, it was brought to international attention by the American explorer Hiram Bingham in 1911.

17. B) The Maya

18. Jordan

19. The Great Wall of China

20. A) As a tomb. It was built by the Mughal emperor Shah Jahan in 1632 to house the remains of his favourite wife, Mumtaz Mahal.

Quiz 10 Silhouette Countries

1. B) Australia

2. A) Brazil

3. C) Egypt

4. A) Japan

5. B) Mexico

6. B) Spain

7. C) Qatar

8. A) Chile

9. C) Kenya

10. A) Vietnam

11. B) New Zealand

12. C) Norway

13. A) Germany

14. A) Canada

15. B) Turkey

Quiz 11 General Travel Knowledge

1. Death Valley

2. Romulus and Remus

3. C) Dubai, UAE

4. B) Magellan. He gave it then name because, when he became the first European to encounter it on his round-the-world journey of 1520, it seemed very peaceful. It wouldn't stay that way for long.

5. B) Antarctica, at the Vostok Research Station in 1983.

6. Prado

Answers

7. A) The Andes at around 8900km (5500 miles). It's dwarfed, however, by the undersea Mid-Ocean Ridge, which extends across the Earth for over 65,000km (40,400 miles).

8. Yen

9. B) Four

10. Mandarin

11. Denmark

12. Saigon

13. B) Mexico City (with around 21.6 million people, compared with 8.2 million in New York and 6.3 million in Toronto)

14. B) Tanzania

15. Diwali

16. Dugongs

17. A) Veld

18. South America

19. C) Utah

20. Sir Christopher Wren

Quiz 12 Central and East Asia

1. A) Land

2. Kazakhstan

3. The Gobi Desert

4. A) A spaceport for launching rockets. It's the Baikonur Cosmodrome from where most Russian space missions are launched.

5. B) 1988

6. C) Tajikistan

7. Taipei 101

8. Turkmenistan

9. C) A tent, widely used by the country's large nomadic population

10. B) Mongolia

11. South Korea

12. The Yangtze

13. C) Uzbekistan

14. B) Gates of Hell

15. North Korea. They depict the former presidents Kim Il Sung and Kim Jong Il of the isolated socialist state.

16. The Silk Road

17. A) A stew of rice, meat and vegetables.

Answers

18. Nur-Sultan. It was named after the country's former president, Nursultan Nazarbayev, who ruled as Kazakhstan's dictator from 1991 to 2019.

19. Ming. Although it was started over 2000 years ago, most of the best-preserved sections of the Wall date from the time of the Ming Dynasty (1368-1644).

20. C) They never have. Although the conflict ended with an armistice in 1953, the two countries didn't sign a peace treaty, meaning they are still technically at war.

Quiz 13 **London**

1. B) 1963 (when it was finally overtaken by the 118m (387ft) Millbank Tower

2. A) The Shard at 310m (1016ft)

3. Beefeaters

4. B) British Museum

5. C) Blue (light blue to be exact)

6. C) The Crystal Palace. It was erected in Hyde Park and later moved to South London where a district still bears its name (though the structure itself burnt down in 1936).

7. A) A fruit, vegetable and flower market, as frequented by the likes of Eliza Doolittle in *Pygmalion*.

8. B) King's Cross

9. B) Regent's Park

10. Red

11. A) The Millennium

12. A) Trafalgar Square

13. B) The Elizabeth Tower. It was originally simply called The Clock Tower, but the name was changed in 2012 in honour of Queen Elizabeth II's Diamond Jubilee.

14. 1666

15. A) The Palace of Westminster

16. B) Gatwick

17. Bloomsbury. It was the Bloomsbury Group.

18. Oxford Street

19. Cricket

20. The Savoy

Answers

Quiz 14 Bridges

1. B) 400 (which span around 150 canals)

2. Manhattan

3. Tower Bridge

4. C) Turkey. It's the 1915 Çanakkale Bridge, which was built to commemorate a Turkish victory over British and Australian troops in the First World War, and has a main span measuring 2023m (6637ft).

5. A) Cast Iron. It still stands today over the River Severn in the English county of Shropshire.

6. B) China. It's the Danyang-Kunshan Grand Bridge, a 164.8km (102.4 mile) viaduct carrying a stretch of the Beijing–Shanghai High-Speed Railway.

7. A) Charles Bridge

8. A) O. This is both because the river is un-spannably wide in places and because it's mainly fringed by thick rainforest that would make bridge construction too difficult.

9. Johannesburg

10. C) International Orange. Widely used in the aeronautics industry, the colour was chosen because it's highly visible in fog, which is common in San Francisco Bay where the bridge is located.

11. C) 18th century (not till 1750 to be exact. Until recent times, most crossings of the river were made by boat).

12. The George Washington Bridge

13. A) A rail bridge. The nearby road bridge is officially known as the Forth Road Bridge.

14. 1930s (1932 to be exact)

15. B) Florence

16. A) Egypt. It's a 20.5km (12.7 mile) elevated highway connecting Cairo City with the International Airport.

17. B) 565m (1854ft). Opened in 2016, it's perched on hills either side of the Beipan River.

18. A) Circular. Its distinctive shape supposedly makes drivers slow down while crossing the bridge.

19. B) It's the world's tallest bridge (measured from ground level) at 336.4 m (1,104ft)

20. Arizona

Answers

Quiz 15 **Waterfalls**

1. C) 979m (3212ft)

2. B) Venezuela

3. He discovered them in the 1930s (1933) while flying a small plane on the lookout for a bed of gold ore.

4. A) South Africa

5. C) Zambezi

6. Argentina

7. B) Throat

8. B) Bridal Veil Falls

9. C) Marilyn Monroe

10. B) They are human-made, and very old. The 165m (541ft) falls were originally created by the ancient Romans in the third century BCE by diverting water from a wetland along a canal off a nearby cliff.

11. A) Australia. They are 268m (879ft) high.

12. B) Malham Cove is now a dried up waterfall, But, after heavy rains in 2015, water fell here for the first time since 1824.

13. A) Norway

14. C) Hawaii

15. B) Latvia. At up to 270m (886ft) acrpss, it is very wide, but only dropping down a maximum 2.2m (7ft), it's not very high.

16. C) Fall of Snow

17. B) Honduras

18. A) The Fang

19. C) The Dominican Republic

20. A) Cameroon

Quiz 16 **General Travel Knowledge**

1. C) Italy

2. B) Belize. It was formerly the colony of British Honduras.

3. A) Cyprus. The wine has been made since at least the 12th century.

4. C) Tree bark

5. B) Argentina

6. A) Eritrean nafka

7. C) Portugal

8. C) Land of Fire

9. Iceland

10. A) Zimbabwe

Answers

11. C) Zambia

12. Bolivia

13. C) It was the site of numerous nuclear tests conducted by the USA during the 1940s and 50s and is still off-limits.

14. The Rialto Bridge

15. C) Six (split over consecutive weekends)

16. C) Mexico. It's the Great Pyramid of Cholula, which was built between the 3rd and the 9th century CE.

17. A) Cedar

18. France

19. C) Herring

20. It's in the Atlantic Ocean; the nearest country is South Africa; and it is an overseas territory of the United Kingdom.

Quiz 17 **South Africa**

1. C) Three. They are Pretoria (the executive capital), Cape Town (the legislative capital) and Bloemfontein (the judicial capital).

2. B) Kruger National Park

3. B) A traditional dish. It's a type of stew, cooked outdoors in a three-legged cast-iron pot.

4. C) Eleven

5. C) Zulu

6. A) Dragon Mountain

7. B) Shark Alley

8. C) Six: black, gold, green, white, red and blue

9. Johannesburg

10. A) Wine making

11. The Indian Ocean

12. Archbishop Desmond Tutu

13. C) A national botanical garden

14. Table Mountain

15. Platinum

16. B) Tigers

17. C) Rooibos

18. B) Orange River

19. J.M. Coetzee

20. Namibia, Botswana, Zimbabwe, Mozambique, Eswatini and Lesotho

Answers

Quiz 18 **Train Travel**

1. A) China. It's the Qinghai–Tibet Railway, which, in parts, is over 5072m (16,640ft) above sea level. It boasts the world's highest station, Tanggula Station, at an elevation of 5068m (16,627ft).

2. B) *Rocket*

3. Istanbul, Turkey

4. C) Canada

5. B) 1960s

6. C) 9289km (5772 miles)

7. C) China. They're the Shanghai Maglev trains which have a cruising speed of 431km (268mph)

8. A) It set the world speed record for a steam train of 203kph (126mph) in 1938, a record that still stands today.

9. A) USA with over 250,000km (150,000 miles) of track

10. Chicago. It's short for 'Elevated'.

11. B) Australia

12. C) The Blue Train

13. A) Tokyo, Japan. It's Shinjuku Station.

14. A) Carrying supplies to the local prison

15. C) New York, USA. It has 424 stations, compared to 270 in London and 229 in Delhi.

16. Australia, travelling all the way between Sydney in the east and Perth in the West, a journey that takes over 70 hours, one way.

17. B) 1863

18. C) Budapest, Hungary

19. *Some Like it Hot*

20. London and Edinburgh

Quiz 19 **Central America**

1. A) Seven – Panama, Costa Rica, Nicaragua, Honduras, El Salvador, Belize and Guatemala

2. C) Isthmus

3. A) The Blue Hole

4. The Maya

5. A) Jurassic Park

6. C) Belize

7. Panama. Known as the Darién Gap, it's covered in thick impenetrable jungle.

8. B) Rice and beans (although the name means 'spotted rooster' in Spanish)

Answers

9. The cryptocurrency Bitcoin

10. B) USA

11. A) 82km (51 miles)

12. C) Quetzal

13. B) Its seas are home to the world's second longest barrier reef after Australia's Great Barrier Reef.

14. A) San José

15. Green turtles

16. B) Sharks – bull sharks to be exact, which can survive in both salty and fresh water.

17. C) Guatemala

18. B) Puma (also known as the cougar or mountain lion. It has the largest range of any land mammal in the Western Hemisphere.

19. A) Dolls. They're tiny woven worry dolls, usually less than 5cm (2inches tall). They're given to children at night who tell them their worries.

20. Nicaragua

Quiz 20 Museums and Galleries

1. The Louvre in Paris, France

2. *The Night Watch*

3. The Museum of Modern Art

4. A) Australia. It's in Hobart, Tasmania.

5. A) Oxford, England. It's the Ashmolean Museum.

6. B) Rome, Italy. It's the Capitoline Museums.

7. C) The Museum of High-Heeled Shoes, Milan, Italy

8. B) The Museum of Death

9. C) William Hogarth

10. The Metropolitan Museum of Art

11. A) Potato fries

12. B) His middle finger

13. Cape Town

14. Bogotá, Colombia

15. B) Salvador Dalí

16. Peter the Great (it opened after his death in 1725)

17. Victoria & Albert Museum, Science Museum and the Natural History Museum

18. A) Beijing

19. C) Shoes

20. B) Manchester

Answers

Quiz 21 **Around the World in 25 Capitals**

1. A) Tokyo (with roughly 37.5 million people in its metropolitan area, compared with 21.6 million in Mexico City and 20.3 million in Dhaka)

2. C) Ngerulmud, the capital of Palau, is home to just under 300 people.

3. B) Camulodunum was the first capital of Roman Britain, although the capital was later moved to Londinium.

4. Bogotá

5. Senegal

6. Laos

7. Berlin. The monument is the Brandenburg Gate.

8. 1920s (1927 to be precise)

9. Mongolia

10. Yaoundé

11. Fiji

12. C) Río de la Plata (also known as River Plate)

13. B) Paris

14. B) Brasilia

15. Amsterdam

16. Trinidad and Tobago

17. Prague

18. C) Victoria

19. Pyongyang

20. East Timor

21. B) Philadelphia

22. Beijing

23. Lagos

24. Suriname

25. True-ish. It was actually formed by union of three cities: Buda, Pest and Obuda ('Old Buda')

Quiz 22 **South America**

1. B) Emeralds

2. A) Bolivia, Brazil and Argentina

3. C) Green anaconda. It can be up to 9m (30ft) long and weigh up to 250 kg (550lb).

4. B) Giant drawings etched on the desert floor. Created by the Nazca people between 400 BCE and 400 CE, many depict animals, such as monkeys, hummingbirds and spiders, and are often hundreds of metres across.

Answers

5. C) A baked empanada filled with stew.

6. A) The Christ the Redeemer Statue, Rio de Janeiro, Brazil

7. B) Suriname

8. A) Chile

9. A) A goat

10. B) A vegetable and meat stew

11. A) Colombia

12. B) The Sun

13. C) Venezuelan bolivar

14. C) Santiago

15. C) Around 4000

16. B) Cable-car system, known as *Mi Teleférico*, set some 3700m (12,100ft) above sea level

17. A) 1930 and 1950

18. C) English, a legacy from when it was the British colony of British Guiana

19. B) Salt flat

20. B) Hot dog. It measured 203.8m (668ft) and was cut into 2000 portions.

Quiz 23 **Japan**

1. B) Edo

2. C) Cherry blossom (*hanami* is the viewing of cherry blossom)

3. A) The emperor

4. B) Push passengers onto packed trains

5. C) It is partially staffed by robots (human employees are also on hand to help the guests).

6. C) 2500

7. B) A dog. Celebrated for his loyalty, Hachiko waited for his owner every day at the station, including for nine years after his owner died from 1926–35.

8. B) Four. They are Hokkaido, Honshu, Shikoku and Kyushu.

9. C) Around 7000

10. B) Yokohama

11. C) Anime and manga. There are numerous shops dedicated to the art forms.

12. A) Inn

13. B) 1964

14. A) Cardboard

15. Studio Ghibli

16. Tempura

Answers

17. B) Macaques. The Japanese macaque is the most northerly living non-human primate.

18. C) Sumo

19. A) Fish and seafood

20. B) Traditional wooden townhouses

Quiz 24 **Forests and Jungles**

1. A) The Amazon

2. B) The Congo

3. C) Mountain gorillas

4. A) Dragon's blood tree. It gets its name from its bright red sap.

5. B) Peru and Colombia (though it could 'technically' be argued that it also covers part of France in the form of French Guiana, an on overseas department of France)

6. A) New Guinea

7. A) Borneo and Sumatra

8. B) Taiga (also known as boreal forest)

9. C) Australia

10. C) Bamboo

11. B) Finland

12. B) Sundabans

13. C) Redwoods

14. A) It's one of the oldest trees in the world, believed to be over 4800 years old.

15. The Black Forest

16. C) Forest bathing – it simply involves being calm and quiet in amongst the trees and contemplating nature.

17. B) Eucalyptus

18. B) *Avatar*

19. A) Kelp

20. C) The spectacled bear

Quiz 25 **Planes and Air Travel**

1. Orville and Wilbur

2. B) 1903

3. A) 1914. It was a US service from St Petersburg, Florida to Tampa, Florida.

4. A) Louis Blériot, the French aviator in 1909.

5. A) USA

Answers

6. B) 36,000ft (10,000m)

7. B) 18 hours, 50 minutes

8. A) It's generally quicker to fly from the USA to the UK, as the plane is pushed along by the jet stream – high-altitude wind currents. In the opposite direction, planes are slowed down by having to fly against the jet stream.

9. C) The Netherlands

10. Jumbo Jet

11. The UK and France

12. B) It's been built on an artificial island.

13. C) Jamaica. He had a house on the island.

14. B) Lisbon

15. C) Svalbard Airport, Norway

16. A) Olive from the salad

17. C) Amy Johnson

18. C) Albania

19. A) Indoor waterfall. It's 40 m (130 ft) tall.

20. Australia

Quiz 26 General Travel Knowledge

1. A) A race between the animals. It was organised by the Jade Emperor, a Chinese god, and the order in which the animals finished is the order of the Chinese Zodiac sequence. The rat won, and so is first, but only after it had persuaded the ox to let it sit on its head while it crossed a river. Once on the other side, the rat ran off, leaving the ox to come second.

2. New York City

3. Gabriel García Márquez

4. A) A star

5. A) Injera. Wat is a stew and teff is a type of grain.

6. C) Judaism

7. C) Short-beaked echidna. It's a monotreme – an egg-laying mammal.

8. A) The Arctic

9. A) New Guinea

10. B) The Arabian oryx

11. B) 1903

12. A) Kenya

13. A) The little penguin

14. B) Liberty Island

15. Pelé

Answers

16. B) Canada

17. A) *Calaveras*

18. C) Tehran, Iran

19. B) Rabbits. There is also a dingo fence, but that's in a different part of the country.

20. A) Geneva, Switzerland

Quiz 27 **Egypt**

1. Cairo

2. B) 6650km (4100 miles)

3. C) Koshari

4. A) Tea

5. B) Seven

6. C) Anubis

7. B) Tombs. They were the resting places of the pharaohs.

8. C) The Red Sea

9. B) Red, white and black (with a gold coat of arms in the middle)

10. The Valley of the Kings

11. A) Hatshepsut

12. Tutankhamun

13. B) Egyptian pound

14. C) Papyrus

15. C) 90%

16. A) 1860s (in 1869)

17. The Pharos (lighthouse) of Alexandria

18. A) Aswan High Dam, as its reservoir would otherwise have engulfed the temple

19. B) Ramses II

20. The Rosetta Stone, upon which was carved the same text in three scripts: Ancient Greek, Ancient Egyptian Demotic, and Ancient Egyptian hieroglyphs

Quiz 28 **Pacific Islands**

1. B) Nauru. It's the world's third smallest nation over all, after the Vatican City and Monaco.

2. A) Rugby Union

3. B) Maui

4. B) A finely woven mat. They are never used as floor mats, but are sometimes worn as garments and have a high cultural value.

5. B) Humpback whales

Answers

6. A) The nine islands that make up Tuvalu

7. B) John F Kennedy

8. A) Although it does lie deep in the Pacific, it was discovered much earlier than 1979, having been inhabited for at least 2000 years. With parts of it lying just west of the International Date Line, it holds the world's first New Year's party and its territory sits in all four hemispheres: North, South, East and West.

9. A) A ring-shaped coral island encircling a lagoon. They form when coral grows around the edge of a volcano that has risen out of the water. Over time, the volcano sinks back below the waves, leaving the ring of coral as an atoll.

10. C) Bungee jumping.

11. C) 300

12. The left. The country switched from driving on the right in 2009.

13. B) Leis

14. B) Fruit. They're fruit bats.

15. C) Bread

16. B) Guano deposits, which contained high levels of nitrogen, phosphate and potassium, making it a great fertiliser. Sales briefly made the country one of the richest in the world per capita in the 1980s. But the guano supplies soon ran out, and so did the money.

17. C) Federated States of Micronesia

18. B) Giant stone discs

19. A) Coral

20. A) Coconut crab. It can grow up to 1m (3ft) across and weigh 4kg (9lb).

Quiz 29 Languages

1. C) 7000

2. B) English, with by 1.13 billion speakers, followed by Mandarin with 1.1 billion and Hindi with 615 million (including second-language speakers for all)

3. A) Fourth with 534 million speakers

4. B) 40%

5. C) Papua New Guinea. Its many forests and mountains have led many communities to become isolated, developing their own languages.

6. A) To greet someone

7. C) *The Little Prince* by Antoine de Saint-Exupéry

8. B) Swahili

9. Portuguese

10. C) Twenty-two (languages official at state level)

11. C) It doesn't have one

Answers

12. C) Argentina

13. C) You're welcome

14. B) Khmer (Cambodian). Khmer has 74 letters, compared to 29 in Swedish and 24 in Greek.

15. C) 300

16. C) Dutch

17. B) 27

18. B) Excuse me

19. C) English and Russian

20. A) An exit

Quiz 30 **World Landmarks**

1. B) The Lincoln Memorial, USA

2. A) Christ the Redeemer, Brazil

3. C) Arc de Triomphe, France

4. B) The Tokyo Tower, Japan

5. B) Lotus Temple, Delhi

6. C) Great Mosque of Djenné, Mali

7. A) Q1 Tower, Australia

8. B) Space Needle, USA

9. C) Gran Torre Santiago, Chile

10. A) St Paul's Cathedral, UK

11. B) Hagia Sophia, Turkey

12. C) Sydney Opera House, Australia

13. B) The Alamo, USA

14. A) Neuschwanstein, Germany

15. C) Petronas Towers, Malaysia

Quiz 31 **General Travel Knowledge**

1. B) Turkey

2. B) 79 CE

3. Dhaka

4. C) Australia

5. C) Mississippi. Although more closely associated with Tennessee where he had his home, Graceland, in Memphis, Elvis was born in Tupelo, Mississippi.

6. B) Costa Rica

7. A) A dog. According to the legend, the country and namesake river were named after Molda, the dog of Dragoș, founder of Moldova.

Answers

8. A) Jaipur

9. B) It is the UK's smallest city by both population (around 1600) and area: 0.6 sq km (0.2 sq miles).

10. The Dominican Republic

11. B) Red

12. A) Moai

13. B) Namibia

14. A) Tuvalu

15. Tasmania

16. Albert Camus

17. C) Farfalle

18. Spanish

19. Russia and the USA

20. C) Kuala Lumpur, Malaysia

Quiz 32 **Western Europe**

1. C) Monaco

2. A) Luxembourg. Since 1815, its head of state has been a Grand Duke.

3. C) Dublin, Ireland

4. A) Pancakes (small, puffy pancakes)

5. A) 4. They are German, French, Italian and Romansh.

6. *The Son of Man*

7. B) Bonn

8. B) The euro

9. C) Brussels, Belgium

10. Belgium, Luxembourg, Germany, Switzerland, Monaco, Italy, Andorra, Spain.

11. Foie gras

12. A) The Danube

13. B) Eight. They are Austria, France, Germany, Italy, Liechtenstein, Monaco, Slovenia and Switzerland

14. B) Because so much of their territory is at or below sea level. They are literally quite 'low'.

15. A) Cork

16. False. It's Vaduz.

17. B) Antwerp, Belgium

18. C) Johann Strauss II

19. C) Denmark

20. B) Cardiff, Wales

Answers

Quiz 33 **Religious Buildings**

1. False. It's Angkor Wat in Cambodia. Although the Srirangam Temple is the largest functioning Hindu temple in the world.

2. True, sort of. If measuring the entire footprint of the church, then the 30,000 sq m (320,000 sq ft) of the Basilica of Our Lady of Peace complex in Côte d'Ivoire is the largest. But the largest single church building is St Peter's Basilica in the Vatican City, which has an area of 15,160 sq m (163,000 sq ft), compared to 7989 sq m (86,000 sq ft) for the Côte d'Ivoire church.

3. A) USA. It's the Sikh Gurdwara of San Jose, California.

4. B) Israel. It's the Great Beth Midrash Gur synagogue in Jerusalem.

5. B) Saudi Arabia. It's the Masjid al-Haram in Mecca.

6. A) China. It's the Leshan Giant Buddha in Sichuan Province.

7. B) Michelangelo

8. B) In a salt mine, 200m (650ft) below ground

9. B) A fig tree, known as the Bodhi tree

10. A) Ivan the Terrible, between 1555–1561

11. C) China. It's an imperial complex of religious buildings in Beijing.

12. C) Eight

13. B) It's the tallest church in the world, at 161.5m (530ft).

14. Judaism and Islam

15. B) Westminster Abbey

16. B) 163 hectares (400 acres)

17. C) It's still not complete. Less than a quarter was finished when the architect, Antoni Gaudi, died in 1926. Work has continued intermittently since with a tentative completion date set for the centenary of his death in 2026.

18. B) Brasília, Brazil. It's the Cathedral of Brasília.

19. A) Tiger's Nest Monastery

20. C) Casablanca

Quiz 34 **The Amazon**

1. B) Three (Peru, Colombia and Brazil)

2. B) As big as the 48 contiguous United States

3. Brazil

4. C) 30%

5. B) 6400km (3975 miles)

6. True

7. C) Atbara, which is a tributary of the Nile

8. A) Manaus

Answers

9. The Atlantic Ocean

10. C) 325km (200 miles) at its greatest extent

11. B) The black caiman, which can be 4.2m (14ft) long and weigh 350kg (770lb)

12. Poison arrow frogs

13. B) 400

14. C) 8%

15. C) 30cm (12 inches). Eek!

16. False. He wanted a company name that started with the first letter of the alphabet and happened upon 'Amazon'.

17. B) Orange-faced spider monkey – though there is a red-faced spider monkey

18. A) Pink

19. B) 3000

20. More. There are around 1100 species of fish in the North Atlantic Ocean.

Quiz 35 Australia

1. False. It's divided into six states and ten territories.

2. C) Three and five (there are three during standard time, but five during daylight saving time as this is not observed by all states)

3. The Southern Cross

4. A) Murray River

5. B) An orange. It was an attempt to replicate its segmented nature.

6. The didgeridoo

7. Eucalyptus

8. Dame Nellie Melba. The dishes were peach Melba and Melba toast.

9. B) A mob

10. B) The burnt remains of the bails from a match in 1882, in which Australia had beaten England for the first time on English soil

11. C) Northern Territory

12. Baz Luhrmann

13. B) A small marsupial related to wallabies and kangaroos

14. C) Tropic of Capricorn

15. B) Mick Jagger

16. B) It's cube shaped

17. C) Marlborough (which is a wine region in New Zealand)

18. B) Crabs

19. Thomas Keneally

20. A) Opal

Answers

Quiz 36 **General Travel Knowledge**

1. B) China

2. B) New York, USA

3. B) Santos

4. A) New York Cosmos

5. C) Barbary apes (which are monkeys, despite their name)

6. The Netherlands

7. Irish

8. B) A goat

9. Black

10. A) Columbo

11. B) Brussels, Belgium. Brussels airport is the world's largest chocolate retailer, selling more than 2 tonnes of the confectionery every day.

12. Alaska

13. Emperor Haile Selassie of Ethiopia

14. Elba (from 1814 to 1815, when he escaped) and Saint Helena (from 1815 till his death in 1821)

15. Vanuatu

16. C) Both the UK and France. The two powers jointly ruled the territory.

17. Burkina Faso

18. A) Man of the forest

19. The Red Crescent

20. B) Africa

Quiz 37 **Boats and Ships**

1. B) Southampton, England. The ship was built in Belfast, Northern Ireland, and stopped off in Cherbourg en route to what would have been her maiden voyage to New York, had an iceberg not intervened.

2. B) An extra float on the side of the hull providing stability

3. A) Tea

4. C) The hovercraft

5. C) HMS *Endeavour*

6. Plato. He used the term in Book VI of his *Republic*.

7. Thor Heyerdahl. He was attempting to prove that the islands of the South Pacific were settled by colonisers from South America. Although his voyage was successful, it's now generally accepted that the islands were settled from the other direction, from Southeast Asia.

8. C) 1980s (in 1982)

Answers

9. B) Portsmouth

10. The *Pequod*

11. B) 300, which is about 155m (510ft) long

12. Pea green

13. B) Viking ships

14. A) Fifteen ('Yo-ho-ho and a bottle of rum')

15. A) The bottom of the Mariana Trench. The submersible has journeyed to the five deepest points in the world's oceans.

16. *The Dawn Treader*

17. HMS *Beagle*

18. *Jaws*

19. B) Ernest Shackleton

20. A) *Black Pig*

Quiz 38 **The Caribbean**

1. B) Bridgetown

2. Jamaica

3. C) Mint

4. B) It has the world's shortest commercial runway. It's just 400m (1312ft) long and can only be used by propeller-powered planes, not jets.

5. Puerto Rico

6. A) Six. On average, 13 named storms hit the Caribbean each year – storms are named when winds hit 60kph (37 mph) – of which around six will reach the necessary wind speed to be classed as hurricanes: 120kph (75mph).

7. A) Magnificent frigatebird

8. Haiti

9. A) Jerk

10. The UK

11. B) Two: Puerto Rico and the US Virgin Islands

12. Barbados

13. B) France

14. C) Trinidad and Tobago

15. B) Flying fish and coucou

16. C) 32

17. Grenada

18. Cuba

19. A) Saint Kitts and Nevis

20. B) Red Stripe beer

Answers

Quiz 39 **Film Locations Around the World**

1. C) Mount Rushmore

2. New Zealand

3. B) *Deliverance*

4. *The French Lieutenant's Woman*

5. A) Maryland

6. C) Seoul, South Korea

7. C) USA. It was filmed in Hollywood during the Second World War when overseas filming was impossible, but it was set in Morocco.

8. C) Rio de Janeiro, Brazil

9. B) Turin

10. Tunisia

11. A) New Zealand

12. Brighton

13. C) Peru

14. A) San Francisco

15. B) Mumbai

16. The Statue of Liberty

17. C) Caspian Sea

18. C) Tokyo, Japan

19. Zubrowka

20. Bruges. The film is *In Bruges*.

Quiz 40 **Seas and Oceans**

1. The Pacific Ocean

2. The Arctic Ocean

3. The Mariana Trench

4. B) 10,935m (35,876ft)

5. A) The Dead Sea

6. A) The Caspian Sea

7. B) The Dead Sea (it's the lowest and the saltiest).

8. The Red Sea

9. The Panama Canal

10. On the Moon

11. The Pacific, the Atlantic and the Arctic

12. C) Charles Lindbergh

13. The Indian Ocean

Answers

14. False. It's the Bass Strait. The Tasman Sea separates Australia from New Zealand.

15. The Arctic Ocean

16. B) John Masefield. They're the first words of *Sea Fever* (1902).

17. B) The Silver Sea

18. A) Middle of the Earth

19. A) It doesn't have any borders. Part of the North Atlantic Ocean, its borders are set by spiralling currents.

20. The Arctic Ocean

Quiz 41 **True or False?**

1. False, although Scotland's national animal is the equally unreal unicorn.

2. True. Cleopatra died in 30 BCE, or just over 2000 years ago. The Great Pyramid was completed over 2500 years before that in around 2570 BCE.

3. False. This has been a 'fact' since before people went up into Space, but it's not true. The wall may be long, but it's not very wide, making it no more visible than a road or river, which can't be seen from space with the naked eye either.

4. True. The Moon's diameter is 3475km (2159 miles) while 4,662km (2897 miles) is the maximum distance across the USA's lower 48 states.

5. False. The Channel Tunnel is 50.5km (31.3 miles) long, but it's beaten by the Gotthard Base Tunnel in Switzerland, which its 57.1km (35.5 miles) long.

6. True. People weren't risked until subsequent flights.

7. False. It takes seven days (eight nights) – still quite a long journey.

8. False. It's more like a third.

9. False. The Kola Superdeep Borehole, which was dug in Russia in the 1980s, only made it down to around 12,262m down (40,230ft), which is only around one 530th of the distance to the Earth's centre.

10. False. France is the world's most visited country.

11. True

12. False. Just 3% of Earth's water is fresh.

13. True. Their name comes for the Latin *Canariae Insulae* meaning 'Island of Dogs' (although the 'dogs' may actually have been seals). The birds were named after the islands.

14. False. There are three countries: USA, Liberia and Myanmar (Burma).

15. False. It's the world's wettest place, receiving over 10m (32ft) of rain a year.

16. False. It's the Venetian, a Venice-themed hotel in Las Vegas, USA.

17. True

18. True. There are over 260,000 of them.

Answers

19. False, although it's close. Only 12 people have been to the Moon, but over 20 have been to the bottom of Earth's ocean. Many more people have been into space, however – around 600 and counting.

20. False. It's more like 7%.

21. True. At least 64% of all New Zealand homes have at least one pet.

22. False, although it's only been classed as an alcoholic drink since 2013

23. False. It's the opposite way round. The Moon is gradually moving further away, weakening its gravitational pull and increasing the day length on Earth by just under two milliseconds a century.

24. False. It's known as a laguar or lepjag.

25. True. They're all tropical storms. Their name depends on where they occur. Hurricanes form over the North Atlantic Ocean and Northeast Pacific. Cyclones form over the South Pacific and Indian Ocean, while typhoons form over the Northwest Pacific Ocean.

Quiz 42 **West Africa**

1. B) 16

2. A) French

3. B) Portuguese

4. C) Mauritania

5. B) 500. English is the official language.

6. A) A sauropod, like diplodocus, with a long neck

7. A) Mali

8. A) 1957, making it the first African country to break free of British rule

9. B) 22

10. C) Freetown

11. B) Liberia

12. C) He may have been the richest person who ever lived, having built up a vast fortune from his territory's gold mines. Some estimates put his fortune at around $400 billion in today's money.

13. B) '7 Seconds'

14. Côte d'Ivoire

15. Nigeria (with an estimated population of 211 million)

16. A) Secretary General of the United Nations

17. The River Niger

18. A) Benin

19. B) Ghana

20. A) Liberia

Answers

Quiz 43 Castles, Palaces and Fortresses

1. A) Sintra

2. A) Wales. It has around 600 castles spread across 20,000 sq km of territory, or one for every 33 sq km.

3. B) Saint Petersburg

4. C) The Red Fort, Delhi

5. C) Kronborg Castle, Helsingør, Denmark

6. B) Ethiopia

7. B) Louis XIV

8. B) Stone houses

9. Forbidden City, Beijing, China

10. Venice

11. A) White. It is also known as the 'White Heron Castle'

12. C) Poland

13. B) Windsor Castle

14. A) Third millennium (in around 2500 BCE)

15. A) Ottoman

16. B) Hawaii. It's the Iolani Palace, which was home to the rulers of the Kingdom of Hawaii until the overthrow of the monarchy in 1893.

17. C) Buddha

18. A) Pink. It's the Casa Rosada.

19. C) Bran Castle

20. B) Palace of the Winds

Quiz 44 Sydney

1. B) 1788

2. B) New South Wales

3. C) The Coathanger

4. A) Tyne Bridge, Newcastle

5. B) Sydneysiders

6. B) 1973

7. C) Danish

8. A) Sydney Swans

9. Hugh Jackman

10. A) *Sydney Morning Herald*

11. B) 20%. There are around 25 million people in the whole of Australia, and around 5 million of them live in Sydney

12. C) Bate Bay

Answers

13. True

14. 2000

15. C) Sydney Tower

16. B) The Australian Museum

17. A) Two (three during daylight saving time from October to March)

18. C) 100

19. C) AC/DC

20. A) The pacemaker

Quiz 45 **Deserts**

1. B) 25cm (10 inches)

2. B) Antarctica. Although we often think of deserts as hot places, there are cold deserts too, and Antarctica is the coldest. It receives very little precipitation each year in the form of snow, but what it does get doesn't melt and slowly builds up to form the continent's great icy expanse.

3. A) Atacama Desert

4. China and Mongolia

5. A) Angola

6. India

7. A) Mexico

8. C) Mozambique

9. B) Great Thirst

10. C) China

11. Europe

12. B) Great Basin Desert

13. Africa

14. A) Arabian Desert

15. Namib Desert

16. B) 18%

17. C) Great Victoria Desert

18. North America

19. A) Gobi Desert, which is technically classed as a cold desert

20. B) Iran

Quiz 46 **France**

1. B) 14 July

2. C) The Loire

3. A) The World

Answers

4. The franc
5. B) Red, white and blue
6. C) *Fraternité*
7. C) Red polka dots
8. A) *Poisson d'Avril* (April Fish)
9. B) Louis XVI
10. 1789
11. B) Delacroix
12. *Les Misérables*
13. B) Marseille
14. C) Champagne
15. Mont Blanc
16. Notre-Dame
17. Switzerland. The French name for the lake is Lac Léman.
18. Edith Piaf
19. B) Parc Astérix
20. A) Dix Pour Cent

Quiz 47 **The Wide World of Sports**
1. Athens, Greece
2. C) Sumo
3. C) 23
4. England and Australia
5. Barcelona, Napoli and Sevilla
6. The New England Patriots and the Tampa Bay Buccaneers
7. Roger Federer, Stan Wawrinka, Martina Hingis
8. Japan and South Korea
9. Augusta. It's the Masters Tournament.
10. B) Jamaica
11. England, Scotland, Wales, Ireland, France and Italy
12. Detroit
13. B) Reykjavík, Iceland
14. C) Madison Square Garden
15. C) The America's Cup. The sailing trophy was first awarded in 1851.
16. A) Wembley Stadium, London, England
17. Australia (Australian Open), France (French Open), England (Wimbledon), USA (US Open)
18. London

Answers

19. B) Rugby Union

20. Ukraine

Quiz 48 **Explorers and Voyages of Discovery**

1. A) Leif Erikson (in around 1000 CE)

2. B) Fabian Gottlieb von Bellinghausen. He was a Russian naval officer, who led the first expedition to definitively see the continent of Antarctica in 1820.

3. B) Apollo 11

4. *Around the World in Eighty Days* by Jules Verne

5. B) 55 BCE

6. B) *Golden Hind*

7. C) Tanzania

8. B) 15th

9. A) Hawaii

10. Portuguese (though in the service of Spain)

11. C) Wisconsin

12. True. It was named in 1865 in honour of George Everest, a former British Surveyor General of India, who had never (and would never) see the mountain.

13. Tenzing Norgay

14. The Louisiana Purchase

15. B) The Atlantic Ocean

16. B) El Dorado

17. A) The North Pole. He and fellow explorer Robert Peary claimed they had reached the Pole in 1909, but subsequent investigations have suggested their calculations may have been slightly off.

18. A) New Zealand. It wasn't settled until the 14th century, making it the last substantial landmass to be colonised by people.

19. Captain Bligh

20. B) *The Million* (*Il Milione* in Italian). In English, the book is usually called *The Book of Marvels*, or simply *The Travels of Marco Polo.*

Quiz 49 **Southeast Asia**

1. C) Eleven

2. C) Indonesia

3. C) Indonesia

4. B) Singapore

5. A) Brunei

6. A) Manila, Philippines

Answers

7. Malaysia, Indonesia and Brunei

8. A) The Baht

9. Phnom Penh

10. In Myanmar (Burma). It's the Kyaiktiyo Pagoda and is supposedly held in place by a single hair from the Buddha's head.

11. C) Cashew

12. B) Coconut oil

13. Krakatoa

14. A) Vietnam

15. Kuala Lumpur, Malaysia

16. A) Mekong

17. C) Pho

18. A) A primate

19. Myanmar (Burma), China, Vietnam, Cambodia and Thailand

20. C) 17,000

Quiz 50 Silhouette Cities

1. B) Cape Town, South Africa

2. A) Berlin, Germany

3. A) Tokyo, Japan

4. B) Washington DC, USA

5. C) Athens, Greece

6. A) Delhi, India

7. A) Venice, Italy

8. B) Vancouver, Canada

9. B) Prague, Czech Republic

10. C) Sydney, Australia

11. A) Singapore

12. B) Rome, Italy

13. C) Buenos Aires

14. A) Istanbul, Turkey

15. B) Hong Kong, China

Quiz 51 Guess the Country

1. Portugal

2. Jordan

3. France

4. Barbados

Answers

5. Croatia

6. Madagascar

7. Finland

8. Mongolia

9. Japan

10. Nigeria

11. Sri Lanka

12. Uzbekistan

13. Peru

14. Mexico

15. Canada

16. Kenya

17. Costa Rica

18. India

19. New Zealand

20. Argentina

Quiz 52 **Central and Southern Africa**

1. B) A plateau

2. A) France

3. A) Okapi

4. B) Society of Ambience-Makers and Elegant People. The movement promotes elegance and dandy-ish dress. Male adherents are called sapeurs. Women are sapeuses.

5. C) Cloak. Early Portuguese explorers thought the shape of the river around the country's capital, Libreville, resembled a cloak.

6. C) Diamonds

7. C) The Kingdom of the Sky

8. C) It's the world's oldest desert, dating back at least 55 million years.

9. A) Eswatini

10. B) A firearm (a Kalashnikov rifle). Guatemala is the ony other nation to feature a firearm on its flag.

11. A) Luanda

12. C) It is home to more fish species than any other lake in the world – over 1000.

13. B) African fish eagle

14. A) Shona

15. B) 10%

Answers

16. B) 4700km (2900 miles)

17. True. It was established in 1925.

18. B) Leatherback turtle

19. A) Blue, white and black

20. C) Angola

Quiz 53 **Monuments and Architecture**

1. A) Vallabhbhai Patel

2. C) Thirty years

3. B) The Motherland Calls, Russia – 85m (279ft)

4. B) Queen Victoria

5. The Centre Pompidou

6. B) Delhi. It's a Bahá'í House of Worship.

7. A) Zaha Hadid

8. C) Prairie School

9. B) France. The sculptor was Paul Landowski.

10. C) Napier

11. B) It was built inside a canyon.

12. C) Edwin Lutyens

13. A) Montreal

14. C) Weimar

15. C) Agra

16. A) Dakar, Senegal

17. B) Crazy Horse

18. A) Reykjavík, Iceland

19. B) 1st century CE

20. C) The Pink Mosque

Quiz 54 **New York**

1. B) New Amsterdam

2. A) Five: Manhattan, the Bronx, Queens, Brooklyn and Staten Island

3. B) 1970

4. *New York Post*

5. B) The Gershwin Theatre

6. A) The apartment block in *Friends*

7. B) France

8. C) Catherine of Braganza (1638–1705), the wife of King Charles II of England

9. C) Landing dock for airships. It never fulfilled its purpose.

Answers

10. A) Macy's

11. C) 4km (2.5 miles)

12. B) Queens

13. A) The Met. It's the largest art museum in the USA.

14. The Flatiron Building

15. C) 750,000

16. B) Basketball. It's the home of the New York Knicks.

17. A) Columbia

18. The Hudson (The East 'River' is actually a tidal estuary, not a river)

19. A) Vermouth

20. Staten Island Ferry

Quiz 55 **Natural Wonders**

1. B) White horses

2. B) 12km (7.5 miles)

3.C) 70m (230ft)

4. B) 20–40%

5. C) 50%

6. B) It's the largest hot spring in the world.

7. B) Pelicans

8. A) Russia. It's Mount Elbrus, at 5642m (18,510ft).

9. C) 45

10. B) Botswana

11. B) Italy

12. The Everglades

13. C) An antelope

14. A) Acacia

15. A) Iran

16. B) Sandstone

17. A) A rodent

18. C) Meadow

19. C) Argentina

20. B) The Pantanal, South America

Quiz 56 **General Travel Knowledge**

1. B) *Ever Given*

2. C) Bridge of Sighs (supposdely because the despairing soungs made by convicts as they were led across the bridge to the prison)

Answers

3. Utah. It hosted the Winter Olympics in 2002.

4. False. It's the pink fairy armadillo.

5. C) Christmas

6. A) Taiwan

7. B) Orange

8. Borneo

9. A) Christiania

10. A) The Ark of the Covenant

11. B) New York and Tokyo

12. C) Finnish, which is a Uralic language

13. Port Moresby

14. George W Bush

15. C) The Congo

16. B) Peru

17. A) Wellington, New Zealand

18. Boris Yeltsin (from 1991–99)

19. A) 1930s (in 1935)

20. England

Quiz 57 **Buses and Bikes**

1. B) Jakarta, Indonesia

2. B) China

3. C) To stand out from competitors. In the early days of bus transport during the first part of the 20th century, several rival companies ran services, all with different liveries. The company that came to dominate, the London General Omnibus Company had a red livery to make its buses instantly recognisable.

4. B) Routemaster

5. A) Tica Bus

6. A) Greyhound

7. C) 90%

8. A) Montgomery

9. A) Stockholm, Sweden

10. B) Haiti

11. B) She was the first woman to ride a bicycle around the world, a feat she achieved in 1894–95.

12. C) Yellow

13. A) China

14. B) Citi Bike

Answers

15. C) Argentina

16. A) Dhaka, Bangladesh

17. B) 400km (250 miles)

18. B) You cannot ride a bike shirtless.

19. B) Race Across America

20. B) 78 days. It was set by the British endurance athlete Mark Beaumont in 2017 when he pedalled around the globe in 78 days, 14 hours and 40 minutes.

Quiz 58 **China**

1. Beijing

2. Twelve

3. C) Between 21 January and 20 February, when the new Moon appears

4. B) 15 days

5. B) The former imperial palace – now a museum

6. The compass

7. A) One

8. B) 21,200km (13,200 miles)

9. B) Sticky rice

10. C) Red

11. Nepal

12. C) 1974 (by farmers digging a well)

13. A) Yellow River

14. B) They live at the highest altitude of any (non-human) primate.

15. C) Glutinous rice balls

16. B) It is the largest in the world by route length

17. A) Shanghai Tower. At 632m (2073 ft) tall, it is the third tallest building in the world (as of 2022).

18. C) 10–16 hours

19. B) Phoenixes

20. B) Five

Quiz 59 **South Asia**

1. C) Varanasi

2. Islamabad

3. B) Holi

4. B) Banyan tree

5. C) Six. They are: *Grisma* (summer), *Barsa* (rainy season), *Sarat* (autumn), *Hemanta* (late autumn), *Shhit* (winter) and *Basanta* (spring).

Answers

6. A) Hinduism and Buddhism

7. B) Peak of heaven

8. C) It is not a largely Hindu country – it is a Buddhist country

9. C) Ranthambore National Park

10. A) Malala Yousafzai

11. B) The Bengal tiger

12. B) 1300m (4300ft)

13. A) The world's highest unclimbed mountain

14. A) Colombo. However, Sri Jayawardenepura Kotte is the legislative capital.

15. B) *The God of Small Things*

16. B) K2

17. C) India and Myanmar (Burma)

18. A) Durbar Square

19. A) Indus

20. A) Sri Lankan rupee

Quiz 60 **Food and Drink**

1. B) Fermented rice

2. A) Shark

3. B) Guinea pig

4. C) 71%

5. A) Cow.

6. C) Melon

7. B) A baked fish pie with fish heads poking out of the crust

8. B) Potato

9. C) Reims

10. B) A spicy curry served in a hollowed-out loaf of bread

11. B) Parsley

12. B) Sugarcane juice

13. C) Goa

14. A) Corned beef, Swiss cheese, sauerkraut, dressing and rye bread

15. C) Egg noodle dumplings

16. B) Mango

17. C) Elote

18. B) A bowl-shaped pancake

19. C) Speights (which is from New Zealand)

20. A) Marshmallows

Answers

Quiz 61 Around the World in 25 Journeys

1. B) King Fahd International Airport, Saudi Arabia

2. South America. It travels between Rio de Janeiro in Brazil and Lima in Peru.

3. A) Darjeeling. It's the Darjeeling Himalayan Railway.

4. Yellow

5. Black

6. Longships

7. B) A motocycle taxi

8. France, in the 18th century

9. Greyhound

10. C) Northern

11. C) The Netherlands

12. Germany. They're the codes for Cologne, Frankfurt and Berlin airports.

13. China

14. C) Australia. It travels between the south and north coasts.

15. C) France

16. A) A bus

17. A) Flying dolphins

18. True

19. The Zeppelin (named after Count Ferdinand von Zeppelin)

20. A) JFK, New York

21. A ship (a warship being tugged to her last berth to be broken up)

22. A) Apron

23. C) 1985

24. A) A boat

25. Australia

Quiz 62 The UK

1. False. Great Britain is made up of three countries (England, Wales and Scotland), but the United Kingdom is made up of four (England, Wales, Scotland and Northern Ireland).

2. A) Ben Nevis – at 1345m (4413ft)

3. A) Severn

4. B) Birmingham, England

5. C) Inland waterways

6. A) 6th century in the *Life of Saint Columba* by Adomnán, although most sightings date from the 20th century.

7. A) Agatha Christie

Answers

8. C) Gloucestershire
9. C) Wiltshire
10. B) 5000 years old
11. A) Red
12. B) The Giant's Causeway
13. B) 3000ft (914m)
14. The Angel of the North
15. A) Midlands, England
16. B) Margaret Thatcher
17. A) Birmingham
18. B) 1926
19. A) 1952 (though her coronation didn't take place till 1953)
20. A) A kilt pouch

Quiz 63 **World Heritage Sites**
1. B) 1945
2. B) Paris, France
3. C) Damascus, Syria. It was first settled in the third millennium BCE.
4. B) Italy (with 58, compared with 35 for Mexico and 28 for Russia)
5. A) USA
6. B) Liverpool
7. A) Three
8. B) Vatican City
9. B) Sydney Harbour Bridge
10. C) Ethiopia (with nine; Egypt has seven, while Cameroon has two)
11. China with 56 sites, while France has 49
12. B) Mont-St-Michel
13. A) Independence Hall, Philadelphia
14. C) Vatican City
15. A) Cologne Cathedral, Germany
16. B) Ten (Estonia, Belarus, Finland, Latvia, Lithuania, Norway, Moldova, Russia, Sweden, and Ukraine)
17. A) Turkey
18. The Galápagos Islands
19. B) Star Wars
20. C) Thirty Three

Answers

Quiz 64 **The Cities of Italy**

1. A) 753 BCE

2. C) Seven

3. A) A public square

4. B) Florence

5. B) University. The University of Bologna was founded in 1088.

6. A) 4°. It seems much more dramatic because it's so unusual for buildings to lean at all.

7. B) Verona

8. B) Pizza

9. B) Lombardy

10. A) The Medici

11. C) Genoa

12. B) 1960

13. C) 2006

14. A) Palermo

15. The River Tiber

16. B) Pompeii

17. A) Turin. It was capital until 1865, when Florence took over, which then passed the baton on to Rome in 1871, where it's stayed ever since

18. *La Dolce Vita*

19. B) Milan. It's in the church of Santa Maria delle Grazie.

20. The palio (or palio di Siena)

Quiz 65 **Volcanoes**

1. A) Indonesia

2. Pillow lava

3. B) Hawaiian

4. B) A hard magma formation that blocks a volcano's vent

5. False (volcano boarding involves sledging down a volcano's ashy slopes, which is only slightly less hazardous)

6. C) 2021

7. B) Ash

8. A) Dallol

9. C) Twenty. It's a very active volcano.

10. B) El Popo

11. The Pacific Ocean

12. C) Tonga

Answers

13. B) Mount Everest

14. A) A place where lava bursts straight through the Earth's crust rather than at a tectonic boundary. The volcanoes of Hawaii are hot-spot volcanoes.

15. B) A volcano that hasn't erupted in human recorded history

16. B) Eyjafjallajökull

17. Stromboli

18. A caldera

19. A) Noah's Ark

20. B) White Mountain

Quiz 66 **General Travel Knowledge**

1. B) The Philippines

2. C) Ukraine

3. B) São Paolo, Brazil

4. C) 227

5. C) Oman

6. B) Australia

7. B) Frank Lloyd Wright

8. Latvia, Lithuania and Estonia

9. A) Nepal

10. C) Czech Republic

11. C) Madagascar

12. A) 1947

13. Greenland

14. A) Unusual rock formations

15. C) Arizona

16. B) Hanoi

17. A) Vine leaves

18. B) Dunedin

19. A) Kensington Gardens

20. A) Gold

Quiz 67 **Mexico**

1. C) It doesn't have an official language, although Spanish is the most commonly spoken language

2. B) Mexican Peso

3. C) Inca (the Inca Civilization was in South America)

4. B) Chicxulub

Answers

5. A) Mexico City's buildings are sinking. Mexico's capital was built on the ruins of the former Aztec capital and the surrounding lake, which was drained. As water has continued to be removed for drinking water, the ground has begun to compress and subside. The city is sinking by up to 50cm (20 inches) a year and has already sunk 9m (30ft).

6. B) Folded in half and pan fried

7. A) Three

8. Guillermo del Toro

9. A) Tenochtitlan

10. California, Arizona, New Mexico and Texas

11. Guatemala and Belize

12. C) Acapulco

13. B) Four

14. A) 1907

15. B) Mariachi

16. C) Coco

17. C) Eggs

18. B) Yucatán

19. A) 1968

20. B) 1986

Quiz 68 Central and Eastern Europe

1. C) Hungary

2. B) The Urals

3. Marie Curie (born Maria Skłodowska). She won the Nobel Prize for Physics in 1903 and the Nobel Prize for Chemistry in 1911.

4. A) Palace of the Parliament, Bucharest

5. B) Beetroot

6. Vlad the Impaler

7. Zagreb

8. Ukraine

9. B) Ten

10. A) Maize porridge

11. The Spanish Riding School

12. C) 20,000 years

13. A) Czech Republic

14. C) Bratislava, Slovakia. It borders Austria in the west and Hungary in the south.

Answers

15. B) Dumplings

16. B) 1993

17. A) Krakow

18. C) Hungary

19. A) The Dancing House

20. C) 123 years. In 1795, its territory was partitioned between three other powers (the Russian Empire, Prussia and the Hapsburg Monarchy), effectively ending Poland's status as an independent country till after the First World War.

Quiz 69 **Money and Currencies**

1. B) 180

2. A) Queen Elizabeth II

3. True – with some qualifications. Around $40 billion of Monopoly money is printed each year. The US government prints around $197 billion in dollars each year, which is much more, but most of this is to replace existing notes. Just $10 billion is 'new' money, so the Monopoly figure is higher.

4. B) British pound sterling, which has been in use over 1200 years

5. A) 7th century BCE

6. C) Electrum

7. B) Fiji

8. B) 1950s

9. A) IBM

10. C) China (in the 11th century)

11. True. They were designed to depict the major ages and architectural styles of Europe without focusing on any particular country.

12. B) Bitcoin. It was invented in 2008 by an unknown person (or persons) using the name Satoshi Nakamoto.

13. B) Pennsylvania

14. C) Pico (the birr is the currency of Ethiopia and the dong is the currency of Vietnam)

15. B) Numismatics

16. A) Honduras

17. C) Iceland

18. A) The schilling

19. A) Mongolia

20. B) West African CFA Franc

Answers

Quiz 70 **What in the World?**

1. C) USA (that's Alaska)

2. A) Mexico

3. A) Canada

4. C) Chile

5. A) Brazil

6. B) Côte d'Ivoire

7. A) Scotland

8. B) Spain

9. C) France

10. B) Namibia

11. B) Finland

12. A) Turkey

13. B) Tanzania

14. B) Oman

15. C) Sri Lanka

16. A) Russia

17. B) China

18. A) Philippines

19. A) Papua New Guinea

20. B) New Zealand

Quiz 71 **General Travel Knowledge**

1. C) Reykjavík, Iceland

2. A) La Paz, Bolivia – though there is some room for argument. La Paz is Bolivia's seat of government and executive capital, while Sucre is the judicial capital. If Sucre is considered the 'real' capital, then the title of 'world's highest capital city' goes to Quito, Ecuador.

3. A) The Seine

4. B) Wimbledon

5. B) The Sea of Azov

6. A) The kuna

7. C) Ice hockey

8. B) Frank Gehry

9. B) South Sudan

10. A) Germany

11. A) New Orleans

12. C) Turkey

Answers

13. B) 44

14. *Waltzing Matilda*

15. A) Saint Lucia

16. C) Belgium. It was Agatha Christie's fictional detective, Hercule Poirot.

17. Columbus

18. The Red Sea

19. 50km (30 miles)

20. A) Burkina Faso

Quiz 72 **Antarctica**

1. A) 5000

2. B) 1911

3. C) 90%

4. B) Desert

5. A) Polar bears

6. B) Seven (France, the UK, New Zealand, Norway, Australia, Chile and Argentina)

7. A) Marie Byrd Land

8. A) Fifth

9. C) −57°C (-71°F)

10. B) Killer Whale Island

11. C) Active volcanoes

12. B) The lowest continent (its average elevation is actually the highest)

13. A) USA

14. B) 30

15. The Aurora Australis or Southern Lights

16. B) A whaling station

17. B) 60,000

18. A) Be born. He was the son of parents staying at an Argentinian army base. Although other children have been born on Antarctica since, he holds the record for the most southerly recorded human birth.

19. True, but then it didn't used to lie at the South Pole. Millions of years ago, it was much further north and covered in forests where animals, including dinosaurs, lived. Some dinosaur fossils have been recovered from beneath the Antarctic ice.

20. B) Australia

Answers

Quiz 73 Dams Around the World

1. B) 16%

2. C) 71%

3. B) 60,000

4. A) Jordan. It's the Jawa Dam, construction of which began in the third millennium BCE.

5. The Yangtze

6. C) Itaipu Dam

7. B) Ghana

8. A) Colorado

9. B) Lake Mead

10. B) Boulder Dam

11. B) *GoldenEye*

12. C) Zambia and Zimbabwe

13. A) Skateboarding

14. C) Tasmania

15. A) Cantilever dam

16. C) China

17. B) A structure allowing fish to pass over and around a dam

18. A) Tajikistan

19. C) Around 1800

20. A) Canada

Quiz 74 Russia

1. B) 11%

2. B)The brown bear

3. C) Eleven

4. B) 87

5. 1917

6. B) Nicholas II

7. A) Romanov

8. B) Fabergé

9. A) A citadel (or fortress)

10. St Basil's Cathedral

11. C) 19th (it occurred in 1812 during the occupation of Moscow by Napoleon's French forces)

12. Vladimir Lenin

13. C) FC Sputnik

Answers

14. B) Ten

15. C) Volgograd

16. B) The long summer nights and the Midnight Sun

17. A) Georgia

18. B) Norilsk

19. Laika

20. A) *Vostok 1*

Quiz 75 **Rivers and Lakes**

1. B) The Congo, with a maximum depth of 220m (722ft)

2. A) Lake Baikal (by surface area, it's Lake Superior)

3. B) The Yangtze

4. C) 50%

5. Lake Nicaragua

6. A) The Danube

7. Lake Titicaca

8. C) Sudan

9. A) Lough Neagh, Northern Ireland

10. C) Vietnam

11. A) 0. It gets much of its drinking water from underground sources and by removing the salt from sea water.

12. The Tigris and the Euphrates

13. Pink

14. C) Georgia

15. C) Cappuccino Lake (Frying Pan Lake is in New Zealand and Boiling Lake is on Dominica)

16. The Ganges

17. B) Slovenia

18. Michigan, Huron, Erie, and Ontario

19. A) Lake Eyre

20. A) New Zealand

Quiz 76 **General Travel Knowledge**

1. Africa, with 54

2. A) Istanbul

3. C) France, whose territories span 12 time zones

4. A) Blue and white

5. C) Japan

Answers

6. B) 13 (Ecuador, Colombia, Brazil, Sao Tome & Principe, Gabon, Republic of the Congo, Democratic Republic of the Congo, Uganda, Kenya, Somalia, Maldives, Indonesia and Kiribati)

7. A) Milan – though it's close. Milan is at 45.46°N, Venice is at 45.44°N, while Turin is at 45.07°N.

8. The Atlantic Ocean

9. Khartoum

10. A) Tajikistan

11. A) White City

12. B) Nepal

13. C) The Fountain of Youth (he didn't find it)

14. A) New Year

15. The Bronx and Staten Island

16. B) Iceland

17. B) France

18. B) The Boys The Boys

19. Bolivia and Paraguay

20. C) Karachi

Quiz 77 **Car Travel**

1. C) Germany

2. B) China

3. A) San Marino (where there's an average of 1.4 cars per person)

4. A) Red

5. B) Toyota

6. C) India

7. C) Black

8. A) 1894

9. B) The people's car

10. England, at Brooklands in Surrey

11. B) A bull

12. C) Kia, which is based in South Korea

13. A) Aston Martin

14. Elon Musk

15. A) 13kph (8mph). The speed limit at the time was 3kph (2mph)

16. B) Cleveland, Ohio

17. B) 1950

18. A) Argentina

Answers

19. Rolls-Royce

20. A) Córdoba (models called the Cordoba were produced by both Chrysler and SEAT)

Quiz 78 **New Zealand**

1. Wellington

2. B) Three (Maori, English and New Zealand sign language)

3. A) The land of the long white cloud

4. South Island

5. B) 600

6. A) Cook Strait

7. B) Southern Alps

8. B) 16%

9. A) Aoraki/Mount Cook

10. B) Waikato

11. 1500km (900 mi)

12. B) Adventure Sports

13. C) Kakapo

14. A) Sheep

15. C) Filmmaker

16. A) France

17. B) A greeting (where people press their noses together)

18. A) Auckland

19. A) Geysers and mud pools

20. B) Hāngī

Quiz 79 **Southwest Europe**

1. Spain with 49 (Portugal has 17)

2. A) Green and red

3. C) 85%

4. A) Lisbon

5. The Pyrenees

6. A) Decorative tiles

7. Barcelona

8. Real Madrid

9. Spain's currency was the peseta, and Portugal's was the escudo.

10. C) Orujo, which is a Spanish brandy

11. B) Squid

Answers

12. A) Cork

13. C) Tomatoes. It's La Tomatina festival.

14. B) Vasco da Gama

15. Portugal, for which 81% of people identify as Roman Catholic compared with 68.5% in Spain.

16. A) Mirandese

17. A) Alsatian

18. B) Catalan

19. A) Tenerife. It's Mount Teide.

20. B) 19

Quiz 80 **The World of Literature**

1. C) Salt Lake City

2. B) Trolls

3. A) Ernest Shackleton

4. A) Marathon running

5. Canada

6. C) Isabel Allende

7. B) 15

8. A) French Guiana

9. B) Baghdad, Iraq

10. India

11. *Wide Sargasso Sea*

12. B) 1882

13. C) *Madame Bovary* (which is by the French writer Gustave Flaubert)

14. *The Alchemist*

15. A) Toni Morrison

16. B) Nigeria

17. C) Peter Carey

18. B) Trinidad and Tobago

19. A) Vikram Seth

20. B) The American Civil War

Quiz 81 **Around the Ancient World**

1. A) Mesopotamia

2. B) Lebanon

3. B) Boiled sea snails. It was later used to dye the togas of Roman emperors to show their high status.

Answers

4. Lake Titicaca

5. C) 27 BCE (this was when the first Roman emperor, Augustus, formally began his reign)

6. A) Mississippi

7. B) Toilets (in fact, they had a highly advanced plumbing and water-management system)

8. B) Shogun

9. B) Bitter water (they consumed the cocoa beans in the form of an unsweetened drink)

10. A) Great Zimbabwe

11. Hadrian's Wall (named after the emperor who ordered its construction)

12. True. They were held from 776 BCE to 393 CE.

13. C) 8000

14. B) Heads

15. A) A hilltop fortress

16. A) HIndu temple (it was later turned into a Buddhist temple)

17. B) Constantinople, Turkey

18. A) Ottoman Empire

19. C) Genghis Khan. Built up in the 13th century, it covered most of Asia but split apart in the following century.

20. B) Aztecs. It was the alliance of three city-states: Tenochtitlan, the Aztec capital, Tetzcoco and Tlacopan

Quiz 82 **East Africa**

1. A) The Seychelles

2. C) Thirteen

3. C) Madagascar

4. B) It is the world's tallest mountain that doesn't form part of a range

5. A) 17th

6. C) Perfume

7. A) Nairobi, Kenya

8. Kampala

9. C) Vanilla

10. B) Silicon Savannah

11. B) Addis Ababa, Ethiopia

12. A) Olduvai

13. C) A dust storm

14. B) A shield and two crossed spears

Answers

15. A) Madagascar

16. Mountain gorillas

17. Kenya with 104 medallists, compared to 57 from Ethiopia

18. B) 2 million

19. B) Lucy. The skeleton was so named because the Beatles song 'Lucy in the Sky with Diamonds' happened to be playing on the radio when it was discovered.

20. A) Kenya. It translates as 'O God, our strength'.

Quiz 83 **The World's Tallest Buildings**

1. The Great Pyramid at Giza

2. A) Churches

3. The Washington Monument

4. B) 330m (1083ft)

5. The Chrysler Building in New York City, USA

6. B) 1970

7. It refers to the year 1776 when America's founding fathers issued the Declaration of Independence

8. B) 2010

9. C) 15°C

10. B) The Lotte World Tower, Seoul, South Korea

11. C) Las Vegas

12. B) The Home Insurance Building, Chicago. It was the first building to be supported inside and out by a structural steel frame, which would become a hallmark of Skyscraper design.

13. A) Algeria

14. A) Russia. It's the Lakhta Centre in St Petersburg.

15. C) Chile. It's the Gran Torre Santiago.

16. B) New Zealand. It's the Sky Tower in Auckland, New Zealand.

17. B) Radio mast

18. C) 610m (2001ft)

19. A) Clock faces

20. B) 75kph (45mph)

Quiz 84 **Beijing**

1. C) 21 million

2. False – that's Shanghai which has a population of 26 million

Answers

3. B) A mausoleum containing Mao's embalmed body
4. B) 1989
5. C) Narrow lanes. They wrap around traditional single-storey buildings and courtyards.
6. B) 15th
7. C) 9000
8. B) Purple. Its name literally translates from the Chinese as 'Purple Forbidden City'. Purple was a colour associated with high status.
9. A) Tai chi
10. C) Seven
11. B) Nanjing
12. True
13. B) 13th century CE, when Kublai Khan made it the capital of the Yuan Dynasty
14. C) 2008
15. B) The Bird's Nest
16. A) It is the only city to have hosted both Summer and Winter Olympic Games. It staged the Winter Olympics in 2022.
17. A) Mandarin
18. B) Chang'an Avenue
19. A) Roast duck
20. B) Two

Quiz 85 **Roads and Routes**

1. A) Magadan, Russia
2. B) 14th century
3. Route 66
4. C) Turkey
5. Hajj
6. C) Because it let Roman soldiers move as quickly as possible, and they were the main users of the roads. The roads were primarily used for keeping the empire under control, not travel and transport.
7. B) Karakoram Highway
8. A) Dead Woman's Pass
9. A) Ireland
10. John O'Groats (in Scotland) to Land's End (in England)
11. B) A scallop shell
12. A) The Amalfi Coast

Answers

13. B) Peru

14. A) 1888, when Bertha Benz, the wife of the inventor of the motor car, Karl Benz, drove herself and her two sons from their home in Mannheim to visit her mother in Pforzheim, a distance of 90km (56 miles).

15. C) San Francisco

16. Chile

17. C) Corsica

18. C) New Zealand

19. B) The Great Ocean Road. It's the world's largest war memorial.

20. A) Japan

Quiz 86 **General Travel Knowledge**

1. C) Nauru. It's the world's third smallest country, over all.

2. False, it marks the last day of New Year

3. A) The Netherlands

4. A) Niger

5. Bioluminescence

6. B) 1994

7. C) Sacramento

8. A) The Arctic

9. B) The Haka

10. B) The Caribbean

11. True. Millions of years ago, it's believed that the Amazon flowed east to west, emptying into the Pacific before it later changed direction.

12. B) Singapore City

13. A) Southern-right whale

14. A) Suriname. Approximately 94% of its area is forested.

15. C) Wales

16. Spanish

17. B) Thailand

18. Vancouver Island

19. C) India. It's the Narendra Modi Cricket Stadium in Ahmedabad, India, which can seat up to 132,000 people.

20. B) The Rockefeller Center

Quiz 87 **National Parks**

1. A) Yellowstone

2. B) 1872

Answers

3. B) 63

4. B) California, with nine national parks

5. C) Australia. It has over 600 national parks.

6. B) Northeast Greenland National Park, Greenland

7. B) Bengal tigers

8. C) Cairngorms, Scotland

9. B) The world's highest waterfall, Angel Falls

10. False. It's in Grand Canyon National Park.

11. B) Turtles (*tortuga* in Spanish)

12. A) Nordvest-Spitsbergen National Park, Norway. It's located on the archipelago of Svalbard, well inside the Arctic Circle.

13. B) Tanzania

14. A) Triglav National Park

15. A) The Gathering

16. A) Tanzania, in the Serengeti National Park

17. A) Florida

18. A) Thailand

19. C) Australia

20. A) 1962

Quiz 88 Brazil

1. B) Fifth

2. C) Nine (Argentina, Bolivia, Colombia, Guyana, Paraguay, Peru, Suriname, Uruguay, and Venezuela), although there is an argument for ten, as Brazil also shares a border with French Guiana, an overseas department of France.

3. A) 1822

4. A) A type of tree (the Brazilwood)

5. B) The Brazilian real

6. B) 26

7. A) A type of tree – a shrubby tree (*Jatropha phyllacantha*) that can take root in almost any soil and thrives pretty much anywhere

8. São Paulo

9. 1958 against Sweden, 1962 against Czechoslovakia, 1970 against Italy, 1994 against Italy, and 2002 against Germany

10. True

11. C) Merengue (which originated in the Dominican Republic)

12. B) 40%

13. B) Japan

Answers

14. False. It's Portuguese.

15. A) An airplane

16. B) Naval oranges

17. A) A cocktail (made with lime, sugar, and rum)

18. B) A martial art

19. C) Schools

20. B) A toucan

Quiz 89 **The Middle East**

1. Arabic

2. B) Tehran, Iran

3. A) Bahrain

4. C) Dubai

5. C) Chickpeas

6. A) A public bath

7. C) Seven

8. Abu Dhabi

9. B) Saudi Arabia

10. C) Biryani (which is an Indian dish)

11. A) Red and white

12. A) A stepped temple tower

13. B) Petra, Jordan

14. False. It's the Dead Sea.

15. B) Yemen

16. A) A network of over 30 water storage towers

17. The Kaaba

18. B) Cotton Castle

19. True

20. Saudi Arabia

Quiz 90 **US Silhouette States**

1. B) Alaska

2. C) Nevada

3. A) Colorado

4. C) Hawaii

5. B) New York

6. C) Washington

7. A) California

Answers

8. C) Rhode Island

9. A) Texas

10. B) Florida

11. B) Louisiana

12. A) New Hampshire

13. B) Oklahoma

14. C) Utah

15. A) Tennessee

Quiz 91 **General Travel Knowledge**

1. C) Brazil

2. C) Pandora

3. B) 1620

4. A) Japan

5. B) Six

6. B) St Louis

7. B) South Korea

8. A) Chile

9. C) Puerto Rico

10. B) Pangaea

11. Rome

12. B) Two (Nicaragua and Dominica)

13. C) A salamander (the Chinese giant salamander)

14. A) Norway

15. C) Idiot Airport (though there is a Mörön Airport in Mongolia)

16. B) 2500

17. B) Brazil (five times)

18. C) USA (four times)

19. C) 90m (300ft)

20. Hobart

Quiz 92 **Southeast Europe**

1. False. It's the longest with 158 verses in its original form.

2. B) Sarajevo (which is the capital of Bosnia and Herzegovina)

3. The drachma

4. Albania

5. C) Nike

6. Neptune

Answers

7. Gozo

8. B) Crete

9. North Macedonia

10. B) Events included running, throwing, wrestling and swimming. Swimming didn't become an official Olympic sport till the time of the modern Olympics.

11. Seven: Bosnia and Herzegovina, Croatia, North Macedonia, Montenegro, Serbia, Kosovo and Slovenia.

12. Black figures on a red background came first.

13. Nicosia

14. Santorini

15. A) A cross (the George Cross, in fact, which was awarded to the country, then part of the British Empire, by Britain in the Second World War to recognise the 'heroism and devotion of its people')

16. A) Socrates

17. C) Serbia

18. B) Monasteries

19. A) Croatia

20. B) The Cyclades

Quiz 93 Mountains

1. True. The tallest not in Asia is Aconcagua in Argentina, South America.

2. B) Mauna Kea

3. B) Three times

4. C) Flat-topped mountain

5. A) Mount Kenya

6. B) 148m (486ft)

7. A) Damavand (it's the highest peak in Iran and the Middle East)

8. B) 14

9. A) India and China

10. B) 3,776 m (12,388ft)

11. A) Mount Kosciuszko (it's in Australia)

12. A) Puncak Jaya, New Guinea

13. K2

14. B) Virunga Mountains

15. Denali

16. B) South Africa

17. B) The Antarctic

18. C) The Himalayas (of course)

Answers

19. True. Owing to the fact that the Earth bulges out slightly in the centre, mountains closer to the Equator are further from the centre of the Earth and thus closer to space. The mountain that is closest to space is Mount Chimborazo in Ecuador.

20. A) Chile

Quiz 94 **Germany**

1. B) 1871

2. B) 1990

3. True, with over 83 million people

4. C) Sixteen

5. Frankfurt

6. C) Angela Merkel

7. A) On an island (known as Museumsinsel 'Museum Island')

8. B) 1200

9. A) Sweet mustard

10. Munich

11. The Black Forest

12. A) The bicycle (except it didn't have pedals; you pushed with your feet)

13. Thomas Mann

14. B) Four (hops, barley, water and yeast)

15. It was erected in 1961 and torn down again in 1989

16. B) Cologne Cathedral

17. C) Richard Wagner

18. B) 15th century

19. A) Stuttgart (for about a week)

20. True

Quiz 95 **International Organisations**

1. A) The League of Nations

2. C) USA

3. B) European Union

4. B) Nairobi, Kenya

5. A) Human rights

6. Organization of the Petroleum Exporting Countries

7. Current OPEC members are Algeria, Angola, Equatorial Guinea, Gabon, Iran, Iraq, Kuwait, Libya, Nigeria, the Republic of the Congo, Saudi Arabia, the UAE and Venezuela.

Answers

8. Canada, France and Italy

9. C) A panda

10. B) The Red Cross

11. B) 1949

12. The Warsaw Pact

13. B) 27

14. B) 19

15. B) Switzerland

16. United Nations Educational, Scientific and Cultural Organization

17. B) 1100

18. A) San Francisco, USA

19. B) New York, USA

20. A) Addis Abbaba, Ethiopia

Quiz 96 **General Travel Knowledge**

1. B) Tanzania

2. B) Prefectures

3. B) Stockholm

4. C) Bangkok, Thailand

5. A) Black Sea

6. C) Canada

7. Tropic of Capricorn

8. B) Indonesia

9. B) 1993

10. C) Monkey (it's the Monkey Buffet Festival

11. Argentina

12. A) San Francisco

13. C) 85 (It's Taumatawhakatangihangakoauauotamateaturipukakapikimaun-gahoronukupokaiwhenuakitanatahu)

14. B) Wild Coast

15. A) Three

16. C) Denmark

17. A) 1969

18. B) Croatia

19. C) Lava

20. B) Grenada

Answers

Quiz 97 **Canada**

1. C) Ottawa

2. A) Toronto

3. True

4. A) Second

5. A) Canadian dollar

6. Red and white

7. B) Beaver

8. C) Wood bison

9. C) Toronto

10. C) 90%

11. B) Baffin Island

12. C) Denali (which is in Alaska, USA)

13. B) The world's largest skating rink

14. A) Mount Thor

15. Cirque du Soleil

16. A) The Canadian Parliament Buildings

17. A) The Cabot Trail

18. C) Albertaraptor

19. B) Tidal range – up to 12m (38ft)

20. Klondike River

Quiz 98 **The World of Art**

1. Michelangelo

2. A) Tokyo, Japan

3. C) Twelve

4. C) Toothpaste tubes

5. B) China

6. A) Chiaroscuro

7. C) USA

8. B) Art Deco (it's an abbreviation of *Arts Décoratifs*)

9. B) Manga

10. A) Málaga

11. A) The Southwest

12. B) Oslo, Norway

13. C) Argentina (in Buenos Aires)

14. B) The jet engine

15. C) Australia

Answers

16. A) Walter Gropius

17. A) Cave paintings, dating back thousands of years

18. A) Mount Fuji

19. A) Frida Kahlo

20. A) Venice

Quiz 99 The Arctic

1. C) Eight (Russia, Canada, USA, Denmark, Norway, Sweden, Finland, and Iceland)

2. B) 4 million

3. B) 66° north

4. B) Bear

5. B) 1909

6. The Midnight Sun

7. It struck the *Titanic*, causing it to sink.

8. B) 5500

9. C) Arctic fox

10. C) Twenty-four (although officially the North Pole doesn't have a time zone)

11. C) 80%

12. A) Red

13. True. It's also the shallowest.

14. A) Polar bears. It's known as the 'Polar bear capital of the world'.

15. True

16. A) Harp seal

17. B) It has the longest lifespan of any vertebrate. It may possibly live as long as 500 years.

18. A) Permafrost

19. B) 10%

20. The Northwest Passage

Answers

Quiz 100 Borders Around the World

1. B) France and Italy

2. B) 14

3. The USA and Canada

4. A) Two (Canada and Mexico)

5. France and Switzerland

6. The Rio Bravo

7. Wales and England

8. Colombia

9. The USA and Canada

10. B) Democratic Republic of Congo (nine countries)

11. Iran

12. Zimbabwe and Zambia

13. Monaco (it's just 3.83km (2.38 miles) long

14. Bosnia and Herzegovina. It has a total land border of 1538km, but just 20km of coastline, or less than 1/75th.

15. South Africa

16. Two. As Russia has borders with both countries, you'd only need to travel through the two relevant borders.

17. B) Mekong

18. The Schengen Area

19. A) Indonesia

20. False, but South Australia does

21. Spain and France.

22. False. It share a maritime border.

23. Cambodia and Laos

24. C) Saudi Arabia

25. A) Peru

Published in 2022 by Lonely Planet Global Limited
CRN 554153
www.lonelyplanet.com
ISBN 978 1 83869 569 9
© Lonely Planet 2022
Printed in Singapore
10 9 8 7 6 5 4 3 2 1

General Manager, Print & Publishing Piers Pickard
Associate Publisher Robin Barton
Writer and Editor Joe Fullman
Quizzes by Joe Fullman, Sam Fullman, Frances Evans and Christina Webb
Art Direction & Design Dan Di Paolo
Print production Nigel Longuet

Picture Credits
Key: p= page, t=top, b=bottom, l=left, r=right, c=centre
500px.com p64 crb David MG, p65 bl Rudy Balasko, p147 Judy Tomlinson; **Alamy.com** p85 Wildestanimal, p189 Pattanasak Suksri; **Getty Images:** p26 SeanPavonePhoto, p39 Alexcpt, p42 Matteo Colombo, p46 Achim Thomae, p65 tl Matteo Colombo, tr tifonimages, ctr Emad Aljumah, cbr 400tmax, p102 SeanPavone, p155 mazzzur, p157 www.fredconcha.com, p181 agustavop, p199 Marius Gomes; **Lonely Planet:** p64 crt Emma Shaw, p113 Gary Latham, p191 Peter Watson; **Shutterstock.com:** p10 Wizard8492, p11 LifetimeStock, p17 Haeree Park, p18 Matej Kastelic, p22 Junior Braz, pp24–25 Uglegorets, p29 LMspencer, p30 Claudio Divizia, p32 LianeM, p37 Elena Odareeva, p44 Alexander Tolstykh, p58 Vladimir Melnik, p64 tl Andrei Medvedev, tr S J Francis, clt muratart, clb doescher, br David Bostock, p65 clt Dan Breckwoldt, clb ksy9, br Zhukova Valentyna, pp67 Uglegorets, p71 R.M. Nunes, p80 Don Mammoser, p87 mariakraynova, p95 Sasha Buzko, p97 syaochka, p99 photo.ua, pp104–105 Yurkalmmortal,tr brichuas, Maxger, Stepan Petrov, p117 Robert CHG, p129 DavidGraham86, p133 S-F, p161 Klanarong Chitmung, pp184–185 BOLDG, p193 Guenter Albers.

STAY IN TOUCH
lonelyplanet.com/contact

Lonely Planet Office:
IRELAND
Digital Depot, Roe Lane (off Thomas St),
Digital Hub, Dublin 8, D08 TCV4

Paper in this book is certified against the Forest Stewardship Council™ standards. FSC™ promotes environmentally responsible, socially beneficial and economically viable management of the world's forests.